About

Glen Humphries is a journalist w
the subject of beer, music and crime. S
and stuff. He could list them all but th
he is kidding. It's three, he's won three awards. When it comes to ...
been a Dragons fan since 1977 (before that year's grand final win) and
adopted the Illawarra Steelers as his second favourite side when he moved to
Wollongong to go to uni. The 1970s is his favourite decade of rugby league.
Heavy leather footballs. Players with enormous masses of facial hair. Black
goo under the eyes for night football games. Striped corner posts. Sandboys.
Ankle-high football boots. Football fields with grassed hills on one side.
Three games at the same ground. Daytime grand finals. What's not to love?
Glen was a big footy card collector and actually had the Scanlens Footy
Locker to hold them all in. Every now and then he wishes he still had that
locker – he thinks his mum might have thrown it out with all the other crap
he left at home. The sum total of his rugby league playing career was four
years in primary school, losing the final in Year 5 and again in Year 6. The
best part of those four years was getting the schoolboy pass that let him into
NSW rugby league games for free. Man, that was such a rort, the league must
have lost so much money by doing that. No wonder they stopped it. One of
his biggest regrets is never being fast enough to grab a cardboard corner post
when he ran onto the field at fulltime.

Also by Glen Humphries and published by Last Day of School (www.lastdayofschool.net)

The Slab: 24 Stories of Beer in Australia
James Squire: The Biography
The Six-Pack: Stories from the World of Beer
Friday Night at the Oxford
Beer Is Fun
Sounds Like an Ending: Midnight Oil, 10-1 and Red Sails in the Sunset
Night Terrors: The True Story of the Kingsgrove Slasher

Biff

Rugby League's
Infamous Fights

Glen Humphries

Last Day of School
Wollongong
(lastdayofschool.net)

ISBN: 978-0-6480323-9-7

For more information or to tell me which league player had the best moustache ever email <u>dragstermag@hotmail.com</u>. If you loved *Biff* so much that you want to buy some more copies then head over to my micropublishing site Last Day of School (www.lastdayofschool.net)

A catalogue record of this book is available from the National Library of Australia.

"The same people tonight asking questions about fights on the field are the parents of kids who asked me today about busted bones and getting knocked out. They don't want their kids to play, but they are happy to see someone else hurt."

Brad Fittler
Quoted in *Bad Boys* by Roy Masters

The Match-Ups

Introduction

If you've picked up a book called *Biff*, you've probably heard of Les Boyd. A player for the Magpies in the late 1970s and the Sea Eagles in the early 1980s, he was the major victim of a league crackdown on the rough stuff. It could also be argued he was the cause of the crackdown too. Either way, he missed more than two years of footy due to various suspensions. When the league was done with him, Boyd had become the poster boy bad on-field behaviour.

And yet the league would also use that to their advantage. In the 1983 season – the game's 75th anniversary – the league ran ads encouraging people to get to a game over the weekend. And Les Boyd was one of the players they used in those newspaper ads; it was a photo of Boyd playing for Manly running below the violence-tinged tagline "Come See Les Let Loose". Yes, the league would rub him out for years for rough behaviour but see nothing wrong with capitalising on that behaviour when it suited them.

The league has always had a strange relationship with on-field violence; wanting to outlaw it on the one hand, but appearing to celebrate it on the other. Biff and brutality have been routinely used to promote marquee match-ups like the State of Origin and various NRL-approved DVDs also highlight the biff of years past.

Kevin Humphreys, the league boss during Boyd's time, was happy with the crackdown. But he was also happy seeing players punch each other in the head. "Nobody enjoys anything more than a punch-up between a couple of front-row forwards," he said in the 2008 The *Fibros and the Silvertails* doco. "That sort of stuff's great."

After more than a century, the league has finally realised there's a disconnect between coming down on one form of violence but allowing another. The powers that be worked out that you can't have a game that allows some people, say prop vs prop, to punch each other but then take action when one of those props punches a halfback. A punch can't be okay sometimes and illegal others, all dependent on who's being hit.

There is a section of league fans who do like the biff, who do look back on the 1970s and 1980s with fondness (yes, the biff was around long before then but TV cameras weren't). You just have to check out the viewing figures of some online videos to confirm that. The various Western Suburbs-Manly stoushes are all up over the 100,000 mark. Footage of the 1981 finals brawl between the Jets and Sea Eagles has been seen more than 295,000 times.

More recent biff moments like the so-called "Battle of Brookvale" in 2011 has been watched almost 350,000 times. Paul Gallen's State of Origin punch that changed everything? That's been checked out 86,000 times.

But the thing with watching those videos, is they only tell part of the story. What's missing is the fact that some of the players saw their careers cut short – either through suspension or the psychological impacts of being the victims – because of those brawls. Others missed the chance to play in grand finals. Some were taken to court and ordered to pay damages. And there's every chance those punches to the head contributed to some ongoing brain injuries.

As well, as highlighting the league's uncomfortable relationship with the biff, that's the aim of this book – to give some context to those few minutes of mayhem people have watched online. It's about offering the full picture, rather than a minute or two of cheap, visceral thrills.

Yes, it is part of the game's history and colour, just like striped cardboard corner posts, black goo under the eyes for night games, shoulder pads and penalty goals toe-poked off mounds of sand.

But the key word there is *history*. The biff is in the past. It's gone, and it's never coming back. With an increased awareness of the long-term risk of brain injury that comes with playing rugby league, you're dreaming if you think officials will return to the days where players could punch each other in the face.

Is the zero tolerance crackdown on throwing punches a good thing? Absolutely. I don't hear too many players unhappy the league has stopped them from being punched in the face. Anyway, for all the calls to bring back the biff, all the ridiculous claims the game has become "soft", one thing is always overlooked.

No-one ever watches a great game of rugby league and thinks, "yeah, it was good but it really needed some players to punch each other."

Because the game is good enough on its own.

1928
St George Vs Balmain

These days, St George is best known for those 11 premierships between 1956 and 1966 – and fair enough too. Regardless of the era to be that good for that long is a jaw-dropping feat. But for a time in the club's first decade it carried a very different reputation. To some the St George side were nothing but a team of thugs who never should have been allowed to join the competition. And one player, forward Harry Flower, would be singled out as a man whose actions showed he had no business being in rugby league.

That wasn't always the case for Flower. For the first few years of his career in the 1920s, he attracted praise from the NSW press; he wasn't the biggest player on the field but he gave it his all. Still, that wouldn't be enough to stop him from being dropped to the lower grades.

He managed to make his way back to the top side for the 1928 season, the one where both his reputation and that of the club would suffer black eyes. That downward slide began in the Round 5 match against Western Suburbs at the Sydney Cricket Ground. Flowers would be one of four players sent from the field – three from St George and one from Western Suburbs – in a game *The Sun* said "Feet, fists and heads were used without discrimination".

Another report said "a crowd of 9000 left the ground disgusted with the shocking exhibition. The match was a disgraceful exhibition from start to finish. Such sustained rough play has not been seen in a Sydney football match for many years, if ever."

In the first half Flower and Western Suburbs halfback George Mason had a set-to during the play-the-ball, with the referee giving the pair their marching orders. Flower didn't seem too bothered by this turn of events; a newspaper photo of him and Mason leaving the field shows the Dragon's face split by a broad grin.

Dragons lock-forward Aub Kelly wasn't quite so

pleased when he was told to head to the dressing sheds. Charged with stomping on the face of an opposing player, Kelly was abused by the crowd as he left the field. He singled out one person in the members stand and planned to take things further before a friend wisely intervened and pulled him away.

Kelly's actions would prompt outraged letters in the paper, including one from the amusingly named Arthur Macarthur. "It is bad enough, in all conscience, for gentlemen members to have to listen to lurid language and misconduct by non-members," the snobbish Macarthur bleated, "without being threatened with assault by players."

The last player to be marched in that match was the Dragons' William Ives, who had made a break but was pulled up just short and expressed his annoyance by punching the tackler.

Flower would end up with six weeks while fellow combatant Mason got three. Ives was rubbed out for three games while Kelly was controversially ruled out for the rest of the season. In Flower's appeal, there were allegations that referee Miller had it in for him. A team-mate had run into Miller in the week leading up to the game and later claimed the ref told him "you have two hard men in St George. Flower is a wild cow." Another witness claimed to hear Miller say "I fixed them" in the sheds after the game. Not surprisingly, Miller denied the allegations.

Flower's stint on the sideline would be cut to three weeks. The suspensions of the other three players would also be reduced; these decisions would soon lead to critics saying the league was soft on thuggery. In the wake of a Saturday afternoon match in August the league would show just how soft it was.

As a brief aside, it's worth noting that in its early years rugby league had its wild and woolly moments. When a Maori side played Australia in Sydney in 1909, the locals thought they were robbed by the referee and abused him as he left the field. The visiting fans, remembering their team had won, leapt the fence and took ownership of the trophy. "Men and boys, half mad with the riot that was in the air," one newspaper report read, "tore down the ornamental fence and clambered over by the thousands." When the referee realised they were after him, he decked a few before the police arrived and ushered him to safety.

A few years later, Glebe was playing North Sydney at Wentworth Park and two players punched on for a bit. After the referee broke them up, one walked up to shake hands, but the other thought he was about to throw a punch and so it kicked off again. That was the queue for up to a thousand fans to jump the fence and fight with a few players as they were leaving the field.

A 1922 third grade match between Mascot and Marrickville saw the referee rush from the field and lock himself in the pavilion after irate fans ran onto the field looking for a piece of him. Up in Queensland, they had their own problems. In 1917, during a Western Suburbs vs Valleys match, a brawl broke out in the grandstand. Fans called out to the players to join in; some left the field, and climbed the fence. Curiously, the brawl ended when a woman clobbered the ringleader over the head with her umbrella.

Things reached a low point in Ashgrove, Brisbane, in 1926 when a referee was stabbed by a spectator. In the second half, the game was getting a bit nasty and the referee tried to take action by sending off a player for swearing. The player instead hurled the ball at the ref, who retaliated and was then set upon by several other players. They kicked him in "a vital place", according to media reports, and punched him into unconsciousness. While this was going on, fans stormed the field, one slashing the referee's face with a pocket knife.

In the 1928 Sydney season, there was nothing riding on the outcome of the Round 11 match when St George hosted Balmain at Earl Park, Arncliffe, on August 11. St George had lost just one game all season and would finish minor premiers while, when Balmain turned up at Earl Park they had just two wins to their name. One of those was against Newtown, the only team that would finish further down the ladder than Balmain.

And yet the game would end up going down in rugby league infamy as the Earl Park Riot, where players would be fast and loose with their fists and feet, and spectators would jump the fence and try to attack anyone in a Balmain jersey. It would also spawn a number of myths; that the riot went on for hours, that various miscreants were handcuffed to the goalposts and that two rival players continued the brawl after they were loaded into the same ambulance.

The match seemed destined to be one that didn't make the front page of the paper until just before half-time, when St George forward Jack Mogridge was clobbered by someone in a scrum. He came reeling out with blood streaming from his nose but the referee took no action. Things were about to kick off right there but the half-time whistle called a halt to proceedings.

The hot heads didn't use the half-time break to calm down; when they returned to the field both sides aimed to get square. "The game in the second half was frequently marred by rough play," the *Sydney Morning Herald* reported, "and it was apparent that the referee (Mick Branaghan) had lost control. That official repeatedly cautioned players but sterner measures were needed to check them."

The *Labor Daily* suggested players were putting up high kicks with the intention of pummeling whichever opponent was foolish enough to stand under the ball waiting to catch it.

Dragons centre and goalkicker George Carstairs had come in for some rough treatment in the first half; in one instance an opponent put him in a headlock and only released the centre when the referee came over.

In the second half he received a few more punches and kicks; in one instance, he looked up to the referee for some justice but found none coming his way. So he started dishing some out; at one stage he and Balmain half Tony Russell were cautioned for trading what one paper described as "snapping punches". It would be these two who would be involved in the flashpoint of the riot.

"It was plain that a fight was impending, yet not one caution was administered from the time the rough-house tactics started," the *Sydney Truth* gleefully reported the day after the game. "Punches and kicks were exchanged each time a tackle was made – and still the referee did nothing."

That was until late in the second half when Branaghan finally decided to march someone – Harry Flower. He had resented the attention Carstairs received in a tackle and rushed to his aid. The referee would later insist Flower had jumped on an opponent who had already been tackled by Carstairs and dug in his studs. Flower unsurprisingly felt this was crap and insisted he merely stepped in when a team-mate was being man-handled. Though Flower would have no hard feelings; after the riot kicked off he would serve as a bodyguard to the referee, even escorting him to the local train station.

The crowd, who had booed Branaghan as Flower walked to the sideline, would soon be further outraged by the ref. Five minutes before the end of the match, Carstairs would be knocked unconscious after being kicked in the head during a tackle. Russell was the culprit; the crowd was sure it was deliberate and, given the running battle the two had throughout the second half, it's hard to disagree. But that's just what Russell did. He insisted he had been trying to jump over Carstairs' prone form when the centre raised his head.

The Dragons coach Frank Burge ran onto the field when Carstairs was felled, and ignored the referee's insistence he return to the sideline. Ambulance men stretchered the St George player off the field and worked on him on the sidelines in full view of angry fans before taking him to the sheds.

The fans began baying for Russell's blood. The chant "We want Russell!" went up, and one spectator jumped the fence and took an air swing at a touch judge before being grabbed and thrown back into the crowd. Both touch judges would later report the crowd had also pelted them with stones during the game.

The final whistle sounded but, for some players, the fight wasn't over. As soon as the 80 minutes were up, forward George Bishop chased St George's Arnold Traynor across the field, keen to settle some sort of grievance (Bishop had earlier tried to land a punch on Traynor and, when that failed to connect, chose a boot to the ribs instead). That was the final straw for the fans, who leapt over the fences and stormed onto the field with their eyes on just one person – Tony Russell.

"The crowd surrounded Russell, and kicks and blows came at him from all directions," *The Sun* reported. "He was in a serious predicament when police arrived."

Officers in uniform and plainclothes police swung truncheons and handcuffs into the heads of the crowd, trying to reach Russell. One spectator who was cracked in the head by a plainclothes policeman's cuffs would later find himself in court.

After five or 10 minutes of fighting, the police would gain the upper hand and bring Russell to safety. Once back in the dressing sheds, ambulance officers checked him out and found cuts, bruises and abrasions all over his body.

Both he and apparent enemy Carstairs were loaded in the same ambulance and taken to St George Hospital. This has sparked a tale that the pair carried on brawling in the back, but that never happened. An ambulance man travelling with the pair said Russell was contrite. Asking if Carstairs was there, Russell said "I'm sorry, George. It was all my fault and I got what I deserved."

As far as the *Daily Telegraph* was concerned, the league had gotten what it deserved too. The on-field thuggery was a result of the league's soft stance on foul play, the paper stated, making a veiled reference to the reduction in sentences the St George players got after the earlier Western Suburbs match.

"The judiciary committee's recommendations have been treated with contempt," the paper reported. "A player's suspension has been wiped out on appeal after he has been suspended for the season."

Two days after the riot that had made the papers across the state, the league met and decided to hold an inquiry where more than a dozen players and officials would be called to appear.

They also dealt with the Flower send-off. When the league's judiciary committee recommended the charge be dismissed, the irate Balmain delegate Mr Savage called for a six-week suspension for Flower. To him, Flower caused the riot and, referring to his send-off earlier that year, claimed he was "not temperamentally fitted to play the game".

He also laid into the St George fans. "To my mind the sport is sinking to a very low ebb when a club has supporters who would act like those of St George."

Wests delegate Mr McFayden joined the St George hatefest and supported the call for a six-week suspension.

"Every club playing against St George during the last two seasons have had players sent off the field," he said. "If the St George players cannot control themselves, the game should be rid of them … I will move for the disqualification of the St George club from the league. The game is getting more like pugilism. These St George players are responsible for putting some of our best men out of the game."

Fortunately for Flower and the St George club, saner heads prevailed. The player received no suspension and the club was not kicked out.

The inquiry a week later was nothing short of farcical, and not just because of referee's Branaghan's insistence that he felt he had the match well under control and it was one of the cleanest he had seen.

"The dragnet of the rugby league to discover the cause of the riot after the Balmain-St George match at Earl Park came out of the depths of discussion practically empty," *The Sun* reported.

The league, apparently keen to wash their hands of the affair and shift the blame elsewhere, decided it was the crowd's fault. Conveniently, it meant they would have to take no action against any player or official.

It was actually Harry 'Jersey' Flegg who put the proposal forward. "Mr Flegg moved that the riot was caused by the excitement of the barrackers and was not due to the conduct of the players," reported the *Daily Telegraph*. "After the defeat of several amendments, the motion whitewashing everyone but the spectators was carried."

Perhaps the only person who got in trouble over the riot was Stanley Ferris. The 38-year-old salesman was at Earl Park on the afternoon of the riot and was arrested on the field after punching a policeman.

He would face the judge in late August, stating that, yes, he did hit Constable Gee, but he didn't know he was a police officer at the time. Ferris said he saw Russell on his knees being attacked by the crowd and pushed his way through. He grabbed Russell by the left arm while a detective held his right and they began taking the player to safety.

"We were successfully conveying No13 off the ground, despite the antagonistic attitude of the crowd," Ferris said.

"Suddenly, I received a severe blow on the head and felt an object slide down my back. A momentary glance indicated a shiny object which I took for a bottle and, seeing a person who seemed beside himself with excitement stoop and pick up this article, I struck him believing him to be one of No13's attackers."

Nope, that was Constable Gee in plainclothes. Another officer ran up and arrested him for assaulting police. He sat outside the sheds while the police helped others, mopping the blood from his wound with a newspaper. After everything had calmed down, Ferris was taken to Kogarah police station and charged. It would only be when the case reached court that police would admit Ferris had been assisting them and the charge was dropped.

The next time St George played at Earl Park would be a semifinal against Souths on September 8, and the police were ready. "The police were taking no chances of a repetition of the riot which took place after the Balmain-St George game, and had a strong posse stationed around the ground," the *Sydney Truth* reported.

"They did their job when they cleared the fans, mostly small boys, who had seated themselves inside the fence, but as far as anything serious was concerned, there was never a suspicion, either on or off the field."

Turns out they might have been at the wrong ground that weekend. On the Sunday, Eastern Suburbs and North Sydney met at Wentworth Oval, where players started a brawl after a spiteful tackle from a Norths player.

Around 100 fans jumped the fence and started making their way to the fight, but referee W Neill managed to settle the players down before the horde arrived. But it doesn't seem to be anywhere near as sensational as the Earl Park riot; some of the coverage of the game made no mention of the brawl or the pitch invasion.

In a postscript, if Balmain's Russell was keen on a get-square the next time Balmain and St George met, he wouldn't be given much time for revenge. Barely five minutes into the game he would be sent off for kicking. He would be suspended for six weeks.

1954
NSW Vs England

Duggie Greenall was a bad man. At least that's what the *Sydney Truth* newspaper called the English centre during the 1954 Ashes tour of Australia and New Zealand. "Duggie 'Bad Man' Greenall", they would write in their stories, like it was his nickname or something. His preference for brutal stiff-arm tackles might have had something to do with it. While the tackle itself wasn't illegal back in the day, encasing your arm in plaster beforehand so as to inflict more pain certainly was.

The plaster ploy was always assumed but never proven. The Bad Man would often play with layers of padding wrapped around his forearm, which was covered by the long-sleeved jerseys worn at the time.

He said it was to protect his arm, which had been badly broken early in his career. But those on the receiving end of a whack from the small 77kg centre figured that to be rubbish; it was surely covering up some freshly-applied plaster with which to wreak some havoc. There might have been some truth to this – on the 1952 Kangaroo tour, Greenall and his "padded" stiff-arm knocked out Australian centre Noel Hazzard in the second Test. After the game, Greenall was in the visitors sheds swapping jerseys and some players noticed the heavy bandaging on Greenall's forearm.

At the next match Australian officials requested the refs made sure the Bad Man did not sport any unnecessary bandaging. Curiously, the English centre chose not to wear any forearm bandages in that match.

Plaster or no plaster, Greenall was up to his eyes in the massive brawl that blighted the 1954 NSW vs England clash at a rainy Sydney Cricket Ground. There he is in a photo on the front page of the *Sun-Herald* the next day, striding over towards the backpedaling NSW player Harry Wells, fists clenched ready to start swinging. Right behind the Bad Man are referee Aub Oxford and his touch judge, trying to calm things down, but Greenall pays them no mind.

He's not the only one in the picture up to no good; off to the right is a huddle of five players having a go. And the headline over the photo reads "All-in brawl ends big game". Well, technically it was referee Oxford who ended things; he'd had enough of the fisticuffs and walked off with the second half 16 minutes old. It's believed to be the only top-flight rugby league match to be abandoned, which wasn't good for NSW, who were ahead 17-6 at the time.

A few days before the Saturday afternoon match, it was clear the British had something shady on their minds. They'd selected Geoff Gunney at fullback, while Jack Wilkinson and Brian Briggs found themselves on the wings. Gunney was a second-rower, while the other two were props. None of them were going to scythe through a gap and sprint downfield; the only breaks they were going to make were on opponents' bones.

And that was pretty much the point. The game against NSW was being played between the second and third Ashes Tests. Australia had won the first, while England balanced the ledger in the second. The series was in the balance and, playing in NSW jerseys, were the Australian fullback Clive Churchill, half Keith Holman and winger Noel Pidding. The Brits aimed to incapacitate them so they'd be ruled out of the third and deciding Test.

Oxford said as much to a league inquiry after the match. "It was definitely the object of some of the English players to put these NSW men out of the game or out of next Saturday's game," Oxford said. "It was their intention to maim certain Australian players."

Despite the rain, more than 27,000 people came out to watch the game. It wasn't a great spectacle; the rain had turned the ground heavy underfoot and both teams found it a slog. The NSW side took a 5-0 lead after just a few minutes and then England drew close with a try from a kick, making it 5-3. Another two converted tries for NSW took the half-time lead out to 15-3; good going in the conditions.

Things went south early in the second half, when England half Alf Burnell picked up Holman and drove him into the ground. The touchie didn't like what he saw and ran onto the field. As players from both sides milled about looking to start something referee Oxford issued a caution. While walking away, five-eighth Ray Price (not that one, another one. An English one) said some unrecorded insult to the touch judge, so Oxford called him back to let him know he could enjoy an early shower.

This didn't sit too well with the Lions, who were convinced the referee had sent off the wrong man (sure, *someone* in the British team said it, it just wasn't Price). From there the stiff-arms (from Greenall and others) escalated, as did kicks, punches and whatever else players could get away with.

It reached a low point around 17 minutes from full-time when Churchill caught a long kick from the English fullback. Burnell was chasing it downfield but, before he could get to Churchill and commit some mayhem, the NSW player kicked it downfield. Not to worry, Burnell thought, mayhem could still ensue – even if his aim wasn't the best. So he got in Churchill's face before swinging a punch, which missed Churchill but connected with the back of Noel Pidding's head, who had come to help his fullback. Pidding gave him one back and a few punches were thrown.

Consider this the straw that breaks the camel's back. Players of both sides headed towards the fight, largely to join in. At this point, a touchie ran on to let Oxford – who was downfield following the play after Churchill's kick – know it had all kicked off behind him.

The early stage of the brawl was the moment captured by the *Sun-Herald* photographer and splashed on page one. The huddle of players to the right includes Churchill, Pidding and Burnell, but there's just a lot of jersey-pulling. To the left, the Bad Man is rushing to lay some fives on Harry Wells. According to the *Sydney Truth*, those two began involved in "a frenzy of punching", the *Brisbane Truth* reported it as "a terrific punching duel". After that point, pretty much the entire 26 players got stuck into it; with the apparent exception of Churchill, who tried to break it up.

The referee tried to do that too, but by then no one was paying attention. They weren't interested in anything he had to say. Nor were they interested in the ball; several newspapers added an arrow to some of the fight pictures to point out where the ball was – a good five to 10 metres in the background, partially obscured by brawling players.

With the players not interested in the referee, or the ball, Oxford decided, "right, that's it, then" and called the game off. That actually had the effect of stopping the fight; it was as if the players couldn't believe what Oxford had just done. They sheepishly pulled themselves out of the clump of muddy jerseys, boots and punches, and slowly made their way to the sideline. Many did that odd thing footy players do and chatted amiably to opponents whose heads they were trying to knock off just seconds earlier. Churchill has a consoling hand on the back of Burnell, who had taken an air swing at him just minutes earlier, while Greenall and Wells walked off together, the Bad Man appearing to given his brawling rival a gentle caress to the back of the head.

When Oxford got to the sideline, league official Harold Matthews remonstrated with him to get back on the field and get the game going again. The referee shrugged his shoulders and said, "no, it is too late". The spectators booed and jeered the British players as they walked off the cricket ground turf, and some returned serve to the crowd with obscene gestures. Both teams shut themselves away in their dressing rooms, but some irate fans began banging on England's door and demanded they come out. Surprisingly a few did – among them the sent-off Price – only for the crowd to brand them as "dingoes" (which is a weird insult), before a team official dragged their foolish selves back inside where there wasn't an angry mob.

With the story splashed across the pages of just about every paper in NSW (complete with a bit of faux outrage), the league did what any organisation does when they want to be seen taking action without actually *doing* anything – they held an inquiry.

On Monday night, just over 48 hours after the brawl players and officials from both teams were called to front the inquiry after being cited by referee Oxford. Despite the brawl involving pretty much every player on the field, just four of them were called; NSW's Harry Wells and Englishmen Ken Traill, Alf Burnett and Ray Price. Even though he had been Wells' sparring partner, Bad Man Greenall wasn't called, a fact that surprised the hell out of the committee vice president Arthur Justice.

"Everybody seems to know that Wells and Greenall were away from the ruck on their own," he said to Oxford. "How did you see Wells and not Greenall? The referee gave the unconvincing reasoning that "on the football field I am not familiar with faces. I go on the numbers."

Oxford told the inquiry he had the impression England was more interested in fighting than footy; he was constantly cautioning players for stiff arms, knees and punches. And that was before the brawl began. But when it started, it went off.

"In a flash there were a number of players from each side standing toe-to-toe punching, kicking and wrestling," Oxford said. "I blew my whistle continuously to break up the melee but to no avail. I told the touch judges to get as many names as they could."

Traill, who was cited for kicking and punching Churchill, insisted he was never anywhere near the little fella. Wells and Burnett declared themselves innocent. Despite all three admitting they threw punches, they escaped with a reprimand.

Price, the only player sent off during the game, was suspended for the following five games for abusing an official. After that, some of the club delegates seemed quite keen to sweep the whole incident under the rug and forget about it. Which is why they came up with this less-than-impressive resolution: "Following the evidence submitted, the general committee sincerely deplores the incidents of last

Saturday and warns the players of England and Australia in future not to repeat those tactics."

Sydney Morning Herald reporter Tom Goodman gave the whole thing both barrels, branding the inquiry "absurdly ineffective".

"Had some delegates had their way," Goodman wrote, "there would have been no cautioning, no motion deploring Saturday's ugly incidents, no warning to the Test teams. The chapter would have been abruptly closed."

The brawl piqued the public interest, in the ways brawls usually do. Suddenly, there was a huge upsurge of interest in the third Test with plenty of people hoping it would all kick off again. The same day of the inquiry, hundreds of people pestered the league for tickets to the Test. They were out of luck; the game had sold out three weeks earlier. The cops thought things could get rough too – they tripled the number of officers at the Test. "We do not expect trouble, a police officer said, "but in view of last Saturday's incident, it has been decided to take precautions."

The officer was right, there was no repeat of the fight as Australia came from behind to win 20-16 and reclaim the Ashes. A week later, the English side would show what they thought of the league's inquiry by playing the meant-to-be-suspended Price in a match against New Zealand. The team manager claimed, as the game was played outside Australia, the suspension didn't count. It was a view that left the league dumbfounded; "if he is going to defy our ruling," said vice president Justice, "what is the use of our committee?" One assumes that was a rhetorical question to which he had already realised the answer.

A week after the abandoned match, the man at the centre of it all up and quit. For Aub Oxford, that England-NSW game was his breaking point after earlier being overlooked for the referee's job in any of the three Tests – all of which went to Darcy Lawler.

"I had been thinking of retiring for some time, because I considered I was not getting a fair deal from the appointments board," he told the *Daily Telegraph*

"When I was appointed to the England v NSW match last Saturday I was in two minds whether I should accept the match or not. Incidents which happened in that match finally influenced me to retire."

It shouldn't have been too surprising that there was a fight in the NSW match – the English side had been bashing opponents for most of the tour. Back in the day, the Lions would turn up in Australia and play a stack of games against state and regional sides. In 1954, the team had their first game on May 19 and finished up 32 games later on August 22; it was a ridiculous schedule, all the more so when you consider the Sydney league competition played just 11 matches in that period.

The English brawled in Mackay, where they had prop Brian Briggs sent off, thumped North Coast at Grafton (where spectators ran onto the field during the fight and police had to intervene) and threw punches against Auckland.

Even in their last match of the tour against Coalfields at Maitland, they punched and kicked their opponents. So bad did things get that the *Sydney*

Morning Herald said it rivaled the NSW-England match. It was also a game where the Bad Man was called out. Midway through the first half, Greenall stormed off the field incensed that the referee had accused him of wearing plaster on his arm. British officials on the sideline managed to cajole him into returning to the game because, hey, they were winning at the time. The referee had been responding to a complaint made by Coalfields captain Dave Parkinson, who later denied raising the issue of plaster. "I merely asked the referee to watch Greenall's high tackles and stiff-arm tackles," the captain said. "As far as I could see the referee told Greenall wrongly."

Though you just know the referee got it right – after all, Duggie was a "bad man"

<u>1973</u>
George Piggins Vs Malcolm Reilly

George Piggins was no stranger to being sent off. A quick trawl through newspaper archives shows the South Sydney hooker was one of four to get their marching orders in a 1967 match against Newtown and then again three months later in a spiteful game against North Sydney (referee Keith Page handed out a whopping 21 cautions that afternoon). In 1972 he managed to get sent off during a trial match against Manly – where the league decided on the revolutionary approach of fining him rather than handing down a suspension.

In May 1973 he was sent from Brookvale Oval in a match the *Sydney Morning Herald* described as "dull". There were so many penalties awarded that the teams took a combined 20 shots for goal (Manly's Peter Peters must have been punished with extra kicking practice at training; he kicked a shocking six from 14).

Two months later, Piggins got another early shower after what has become his most infamous incident – the Sydney Cricket Ground fight with Manly's Malcolm Reilly. It was a bit of a messy 18th round of football; Canterbury and St George had an all-in brawl and Wests five-eighth Phil Franks was sent off and charged with "deliberate kneeing, head butting and spitting at the referee" during a clash with Easts. *The Sun*'s EE Christensen felt the players had taken things too far in general, claiming that "many fans like to see an occasional punch, but they prefer clean football."

Going into that Round 18 match, Manly was sitting on the top of table. The Rabbitohs, on the other hand, were just outside the top five in sixth spot and a real chance of missing the finals for the first time since 1966. With only five more weeks to the finals, this was shaping up as a must-win match for South Sydney.

But few people probably remember who won the game (for the record, Manly did, 31-24); instead it's become bookmarked in the minds of many fans thanks to the Reilly-Piggins affair; largely because of an admission of one of the more despicable things a player can do on the field.

The pair came to blows following a head-on tackle from Piggins in the 18th minute of the second half. They'd had a minor clash earlier in the game where Reilly kicked the South Sydney hooker in the mouth during a tackle and Piggins retaliated.

What lit the fuse for the second-half stoush was Reilly playing the ball on top of Piggins, raking his studs across Piggins' jaw. Figuring it was intentional, Piggins got up and "whacked him", according to his autobiography. The two players then stood toe-to-toe, Piggins grabbing Reilly's jersey at the shoulders while the Manly lock had a fistful of his opponent's collar. At that moment referee Laurie Bruyeres ran around behind Piggins and warned the two to cut it out, before continuing to follow the play. In a reoccurring theme of blaming the ref rather than the players, both clubs would criticise Bruyeres for running past rather than stopping and taking firmer action to stop the fight. Not surprisingly, they didn't blame their own players for choosing to brawl in the first place.

Piggins relaxed his grip after Bruyeres' warning, expecting Reilly to do the same. Seeing an opening Reilly threw a headbutt, which was captured by *Daily Mirror* photographer Warwick Lawson. Reilly put a bit of force into it; in the photo his upper body is bent forward and he's raised up on his toes. Piggins must have seen it coming because he's already turned his face away from the blow.

In retaliation Piggins would spring back and wrestle Reilly to the ground, where the brawl continued. Piggins felt Reilly's fingers in and around his eye. Though he later acknowledged what he thought was an attempted eye gouge might have been accidental, at the time Piggins saw red and retaliated.

"I went straight for one of his eyes," Piggins said in his autobiography, "and I'll swear I had it out in my hand. Ray Branighan, an ex team-mate with Souths who had joined Manly, ran in at exactly that moment and pushed me, and Reilly's right eye popped back in."

Years later, Piggins would talk to the *Sunday Mail* about the incident and add the even more unpleasant detail that "I saw things that looked like tentacles on the back of my fingers as it was coming out."

It's strange to see a league player talk about eye-gouging an opponent as though it was nothing more than an amusing anecdote. People might look back on the 1960s and 1970s and wish a bit of the rough stuff would return, but I'm sure they're not including eye gouging.

In the intervening years, gouging has become one of the worst things you can do on the field, with punishments that fit the crime. In 1987 St George's Steve Linnane copped 20 weeks for gouging Penrith's Greg Alexander. More recently, Souths George Burgess missed the remainder of the 2019 season when he was suspended for eight weeks after an eye gouge on Tigers' Robbie Farah. In the same year Canberra rookie Hudson Young got eight weeks for the same crime, committed on Warrior Adam Pompey – unbelievably it was his second gouging suspension that year.

The suspensions Reilly and Piggins got were much lower than that, most likely because the referee didn't know about the eye gouge and only charged them with headbutting. Having been sent off by Bruyeres, they would both get three weeks on the sideline. Piggins and Reilly would make peace over a glass of lemonade after the judiciary hearing. The person most-relieved about the whole affair seemed to be Piggins' wife Noelene, who was pleased George hadn't lost his good looks. "I'm just thankful George didn't come out of the game with any serious injury," she told the *Mirror*'s Bill Mordey. "George was one of the lucky ones. Some of the other Souths players haven't been so fortunate."

That year, Manly would go on to win the premiership, in what has become the most brutal grand final decider in history. Piggins and Souths would miss the finals, losing two of their last four games and ending up in seventh spot. Because of his suspension, Piggins would also miss the NSW-Queensland match and the selectors overlooked him for the Kangaroo tour at the end of the year.

In 2018 Piggins would reveal he'd changed his tune about the events of that Saturday afternoon in July 1973. "It's something now that you almost regret being part of," he told the *Daily Telegraph*. "It's obviously not a good advertisement for rugby league.

"You wouldn't want your grandchildren looking at it, put it that way. It's not something you're proud of but I guess these things happen in the heat of battle."

1973
Manly Vs Cronulla

Plenty of players on grand final day would love to be as relaxed as Cronulla's Cliff Watson before the 1973 decider. That year the league had the idea that the players would warm up at different ends of the field before running to the halfway line as announcer Frank Hyde read out their names before the opening kick-off.

Down the Cronulla end of field, most of the Sharks are going through a half-hearted warm-up, while some of the lamest mascots you'll ever see wander around them. They're nothing more than a pair of painted wooden shark silhouettes on sticks, carried around by two men in tracksuits. It just looks tacky.

While his team-mates warm up with a few drills and some nervous stretches, Watson is having no part of it. As the match-day footage shows, he's leaning against the left upright, hands on his hips and right leg crossed over his left. If his footy shorts had pockets he'd have his hands in them. *And* he even seems to be casually chewing gum.

The very mustachioed prop looks far too relaxed for the mayhem he's about to take part in. The 1973 grand final has gone down as the most brutal in league history, if only because the brutality is in plain sight (the 1977 GF replay was rough and ready too, but the cameras didn't catch much of it). It was a game of stiff arms, punches, niggling, stomps, get squares and cheap shots. In an indication of how lenient officials were to that sort of thing not one player would be sent off. Yep, one of the nastiest, dirtiest grand finals ever and both teams end it with 13 players on the field.

The league itself can bear part of the blame for the fight that lasted for the entire first half, courtesy of the mistake of bringing the players on the field early. Rather than have them warm up out of sight and then introduce each player as they ran out of the race, the league had the players milling about on the field for 15 minutes. No wonder things went wild. "They left the players on the park for 10 to 15 minutes before the actual kick-off," remembers Sharks lock Greg Pierce, "and then tensions built up so much that when the game started they were released in a flurry."

It was a start that went counter to Manly coach Ron Willey's instructions to his team to avoid the brawling. "We can beat them everywhere," he told *The Sun*, "but we don't have enough on them to win if we lose a man early. My fellows will be under orders to make the first 20 minutes as fierce as possible without getting outside the rules."

Rules? What rules?

The relaxed Watson was in the thick of it that afternoon. A prop who had never seen a game of league when he answered an ad in an English newspaper, would go onto represent Great Britain. In 1971 he would answer the call of fellow Brit and Sharks captain-coach Tommy Bishop and join the southern Sydney team.

Bishop's own journey to the Sharks was a

fortuitous one. In 1969, he agreed to a deal with Eastern Suburbs. He resigned from English side St Helens, filled out the immigration papers, packed everything up and flew to Sydney with his wife and four kids. When he arrived at the airport in Sydney, he discovered the Roosters didn't want him any more – he'd come to the other side of the globe and lost his job on the first day in the country. It was Cronulla who came to the rescue, offering him a start.

"They'd only just come into the competition [in 1967] and I thought 'bloody hell, I've gone from captain of England and St Helens to the worst team in Australia," he said.

Bishop was lucky to still be at the Sharks in '73; he didn't play a single game in 1972 due to an Achilles injury and the club took a big punt on his fitness. But the gamble paid off; the captain-coach got the Sharks into their first grand final, just six years into the club's existence.

The pair of Bishop and Watson would create their share of fisticuffs in the last game of the 1973 season. Bishop would start fights by pushing or whacking someone and then duck off as Watson rushed in to sort things out.

"Tommy would be running around like a little mad man," Manly second-rower Peter Peters said. "He'd start all the fights, and Cliff and their forwards would try and settle them."

There's an iconic grand final photo of Peters and Watson. Watson's forearm is across the face of Peters and it's clear from the way the Manly player's legs have collapsed under him that Watson has given him an almighty whack. "I thought I'd give him one for luck on his chin," Watson told Paul Kent. "It was a payback for when he rolled me on my back."

Referee Keith Page in his whites is staring straight at the incident, yet doesn't send Watson off. To the left is Pierce, up on the balls of his feet, ready to take on the Manly players rushing to Peters' defence. But cast your eyes to the right of the image. You'll see Bishop ducking behind a team-mate, looking over his left shoulder at the chaos he has wrought. That chaos was reportedly started from him hitting Peters in the groin, which is why the Manly forward appears to be clutching his nether regions as Watson clobbers him.

The violence didn't start straight away; the first few tackles after the kick-off were clean. Then Manly's John O'Neil took the ball up and copped a few fists in the tackle. He got up, played the ball and then took a swing at the marker.

From that play, the ball went to Manly forward Malcolm Reilly, who kicked the ball and then got smashed by Sharks hooker Ron Turner. To say he only had eyes for the ball would be a lie, Turner was looking to get even for a Reilly elbow earlier in the season that left him with 28 stitches in his mouth.

"Turner came in from the left," Reilly said in his autobiography, "well after the ball had gone, and caught me full force with his knees right on the point of the pelvis."

Reilly wasn't shocked; he understood how things were back then. "This was payback time …To put it simply, I got my comeuppance. What goes around, comes around."

Reilly would go off shortly afterwards for a painkilling needle in the hopes it would see him through to the final siren. But he was out of luck; after returning to the field he soon realised he was no good (but not before smacking a few people) and he had to leave the field for the rest of the match.

That interrupted the meal of replacement John Bucknall (who had just four years earlier cemented his own piece of rugby league infamy by breaking John Sattler's jaw in a grand final).

"No-one came off in those days – ever," Bucknall said. "I'd just finished playing the reserve grade grand final, which we won, and was naturally a bit hungry. So I had something to eat and was just finishing my Coke when Mal went down."

The 1973 grand final was the first time in four years the decider was shown live on commercial TV. And the viewers certainly got their money's worth. Here's few snippets of what they would have seen, just in the first half.

Bishop sees the referee's back is turned so he hits Manly's Terry Randall with a swinging arm, and runs away before Randall can get square. Sea Eagles' hardman John O'Neill stomps on an opponent's hand as he gets up to play the ball. Bishop throws a pass, but Manly's Freddy Jones doesn't care, he just clocks the halfback with a forearm. Ken Maddison swings his own arm at O'Neill. Watson and Reilly come face-to-face during a brawl, only to turn away rather than snot a fellow Englishman. O'Neill gouges Watson, grasping his face like a bowling ball. Reilly smashes Pierce in the head so hard, the lock reaches up to feel his skull, certain it must have drawn blood.

Somewhere in amongst all that, touchies had come in to report some wrongdoing and Page cautioned a few players, but it didn't stop – not even when he called out all 26 players and told them to knock it off. According to Peter Peters, Page said "there are millions watching this on television, settle down and play football. The next one to start anything is off." That wasn't true at all – Page didn't send a soul off that day, with obvious consequences.

"It was just a bloodbath," said Cronulla's Steve Rogers, who was a 19-year-old winger at the time. "It was a total shock to the system. It was a brawl with a game breaking out in the middle."

The *Sydney Morning Herald*'s sports reporter didn't mince words when it came to describing the first half.

"Every illegality was used in those 40 minutes of the first half and several times play exploded into a brawling mass of players. In one explosion about 20 players were involved at various parts of the field with a dozen milling around one spot. Every tackle in those hectic minutes was loaded with menace and was meant to damage. There were punches, kneeing and kicking as the rough play raged from one end of the field to the other."

Believe it or not, there were a few scoring opportunities in between. In that first half Manly fullback Graeme Eadie missed two penalty goals, and the teenaged Rogers one. It wasn't until the 30th minute that anyone got any points on the board. Manly would be first to score thanks to Manly centre Bob Fulton – just about the one on the field playing footy.

Hooker Jones obviously got a call from his centre because on the quarter the Manly hooker throws a flick pass to Fulton. From there, Fulton runs between

Watson and another defender, before also scooting past two other Sharks trying to converge on him before he reaches the line. He's left unmolested to run around under the posts, making the easiest of conversions for Eadie and Manly would go into the sheds up 5-0 at half-time.

In the second half he would score again, off an Eadie pass that wasn't meant for him. The fullback was passing to a team-mate, when Fulton swooped in from behind Eadie to nab the ball. He easily manages to run around replacement fullback Rick Bourke to score. You know those old movies where it seems like everyone is moving faster, like the film-maker has accidentally sped up the film? Well, Fulton's pace is so incredible relative to everyone else on the field that he looks like he's come from one of those films. He just scoots around and past players with ease.

He proved to be the difference between the two teams, so much so that Watson would later suggest the Sharks should have nobbled him rather than Reilly.

As well as scoring tries, Fulton also stopped one –

albeit illegally. Early in the second half, with the score still 5-0, Cronulla's five-eighth Chris Wellman made a scything run only to be pulled down by Eadie just short of the line. Rogers got a relatively quick play-the-ball and spied a yawning gap to his left and prepared to dive for it. But he was stopped by Fulton, who was still coming onside and made a tackle from an offside position. Unbelievably, Page was right there and yet missed the penalty.

Cronulla would only cross the stripe once, and that would be late in the game, courtesy of the blonde-headed Bourke. And to illustrate how little attention the players had paid to the ref's demand to cool it, there was still rough stuff here, with the game in its dying stages.

Manly winger and sometime male model Max Brown went to clobber Bourke as he scored, breaking his own thumb. "And for 30 years I carried quite a complex about that," Brown said. "I'd never been a real dirty player and, every decade after, I went to the reunions looking to speak with Rick. Finally, by the third one, he appeared and accepted my apology."

The Bourke try would be converted by Rogers, bringing the score to a tight 8-7. But Manly would push the margin out to a try (it was the day of three-point tries) via an Eadie penalty goal from in front. That would take the score to 10-7, which would be enough for them to clinch back-to-back premierships.

As is the case with biff today, contemporary opinions were divided on whether the grand final was great, or terrible. "It was disgusting," Johnny Raper said. "I hate to think of the match being shown all around Australia as an advertisement for rugby league."

Ex-Berries hard man Eddie Burns didn't mind some of it. "Punch-ups are expected in grand finals,' he said, "and the public love it, but there is no place for knees and kicking in rugby league."

Other ex-players thought it was fantastic. "One of the best grand finals I've seen in the past three or four years," said former Dragon Kevin Ryan. "The opening clashes are just part and parcel of any grand final."

North Sydney President Harry McKinnon insisted he's seen worse. "Good, tough stuff. I've seen many games like it when the tension has built up in the week before."

It wouldn't be the last time that year Bishop ended up as a bridesmaid. He would miss out on being named 1973 Coach of the Year by a point, losing 8-7 to Newtown's Jack Gibson. Bishop had every right to feel hard done by. The Sharks' turnaround from the previous season was greater than the Bluebags. They went from 8th spot in '72 to second in 1973, compared to Newtown's tiny climb from equal fifth to fourth over the same two seasons. As for wins, Bishop got the Sharks to improve from eight wins in 1972 to more than double – 17 – in 1973. Gibson's Newtown side only won three more matches than the previous year. Hard to see how Bishop lost that one.

1978
Fibros vs Silvertails

"Good, having a blue early on makes them keep thinking about it and then you beat them with skill." That's Western Suburbs' coach Roy Masters summing up his team's tactics in the 1978 season. A season that lives in infamy for those blues that Wests started.

It's a strategy that worked, up to a point. The difference between the 1977 and 1978 seasons were staggering. In '77 the Magpies finished ninth (oddly Masters incorrectly says in his book *Bad Boys* that they finished last) with seven wins while a year later they were minor premiers with 33 points from 16 wins. The for and against records show the '78 Magpies weren't just a bunch of biff merchants. They managed to score 426 points – nearly 200 more than the previous season. They defended better too – letting in 150 fewer points. But all people remember of the 1978 black and whites was their penchant for punching (they also falsely remember those face-slapping scenes from *60 Minutes* even though that was from the 1979 season).

Footy fans also remember the Wests-Manly rivalry from that year, which has gone down in folklore as the Fibros Vs Silvertails. Any Wests biff they remember tended to be during a match with Manly. But here's the thing; that idea of putting a blue on and then beating the opponents on the scoreboard? It didn't work with Manly. The two sides met four times in 1978 and Manly beat them three times – the biff philosophy failed.

To puncture another biff balloon, there is this popular claim that the fighting in the Wests-Manly match at Lidcombe Oval in Round Seven – watched by 10,931 at the ground – created a spike in attendance for the remaining Magpies' home games as people came through the gates keen to see more of that. Of the following seven games played there, three had lower crowd figures; a Round 15 match drew just 3294 punters through the gates. And that was when the Magpies were on top of the ladder. The home attendance was up and down that year, only spiking in the last two games, when Wests were in second spot on the ladder. It suggests it was the Magpies heading to the finals, and not the biff, that really brought fans through the gates at Lidcombe.

The Fibros-Silvertails story started in Melbourne during a 1978 pre-season match as part of a "Festival of Football" where an Aussie rules and a soccer match would also be played. Held on March 18, the league match was last on the bill and newspaper match reports state around 75 per cent of the 4200-strong crowd left after the soccer match. It's probably good for the interstate promotion of rugby league that they did.

Masters had spent the weekend inculcating his team with the message that Manly thought they were a better side – and better people – than those in black jerseys. This was helped by the words of new Manly signing Ray Higgs as he was sitting in a bus that picked up the teams from the airport. Watching the Wests players board, he said to a team-mate "Look at that rabble of shit". But he was overheard by Masters, who had already climbed onto the bus, and who thought 'thank you very much, I can use that'.

When the Wests players came into the sheds down 7-2 after a tough first half, Masters gave the order to smash the Manly kickers. He'd noted the Melbourne-based touch judges were watching the flight of the ball after it had been kicked and not what was happening in back play; so whoever was at second marker had to race to the kicker and knock him on his arse.

"Ray Masters stepped in and changed the course of events," said Wests winger Peter Rowles. "Which was eventually going to be the course of events for the next couple of years, the style of play we played."

By the end of the game Manly's John Gray and Johnny Gibbs were off to hospital to get their faces stitched up. "They hit me like a missile," Gray remembered. "It was a bloodbath. I remember coming away with stitches in my eye and chin."

Referee Jack Danzey was doing his best but he had to rely on those less-than-helpful Melbourne touchies. "There was no-one coming in to tell me what was happening behind me. There was enough happening in front of me to keep me busy."

As well as Gray and Gibbs, three other Sea Eagles finished the game with back injuries. Wests didn't come out unscathed; Peter Walsh broke his hand, Steve Blyth strained his calf and Wayne Smith and Mick Liubinskas both twisted their knees. And Wests lost the game too – 12-5.

The violence didn't put off the Fitzroy club, who organised the event; marketing manager Graeme Plum was more concerned with the bottom line.

"The poor crowd means we will lose a considerable amount of money and we can't afford to as we are a struggling club," he told the *Herald*'s Alan Clarkson. "However we are treating this carnival as a pilot for next year when we hope to have a Festival of Football both in Sydney and Melbourne."

Fitzroy weren't the only club with money problems; Wests were in strife too – after a disastrous financial year, the leagues club's 1978 grant was $120,000 – $40,000 down on the previous season. The drop in funding saw them release six first graders. "Some of our players wondered where the money for their contracts would be coming from," said Wests secretary Gary Russell. "We told them right from the start how serious things were, but they were very loyal to us." It lent a harsh reality to Masters' tale of Wests being struggling battlers.

Masters would use it to heighten his talk of the haves and the have-nots; with Manly being the cash-rich well-off club while Wests were working-class and living in fibro houses. That talk would ignite a powder keg in the first half of the season when the Sea Eagles came to the Magpies' home ground ringed by a cycling track.

They turned up at Lidcombe for Round Seven and knew what they were in for before they got onto the field. Getting changed in the sheds, Manly could hear the Wests players motivating themselves next door, calling out the weaknesses of various Sea Eagles players. "We'd be rolling our eyes and thinking, 'we know what's going to happen here," said Gray. "The shouting, the screaming, whether they were hitting the lockers, kicking the lockers or knocking them over, you don't know. They were getting themselves wound into a frenzy."

One player who went on the field with a point to prove was Wests prop John Donnelly. He'd been spotted drinking eight schooners at the Railway Hotel the night before (the Masters-imposed limit was just three – enough to get you to sleep). There was also concern that Donnelly, an epileptic who forgot to take his medication while on the drink, had had a fit; something which superstitious team-mates felt left him drained of energy.

So Masters got stuck into Donnelly, looking to wind him up to fever pitch. He ended by pointing his finger at the giant prop and asking how he was going to handle the pressure out there. Donnelly glared back and said, "You'll know how I'm going to go after one minute."

Donnelly wasn't exaggerating either. In just the second tackle of the match, Manly's Terry Randall carted the ball forward and was first hit by Wests hooker Shayne Day. Donnelly came in to help, which meant a swinging right arm followed by a few punches. Randall dropped the ball and went after Donnelly – and then the brawl began. Players rushed to join in, while referee Dennis Braybrook blew his whistle like he was a five-year-old with a new toy – but no one was paying attention. Somewhere in the melee Boyd would rake the face of a Manly player lying on the ground before stomping on his head.

When the dust settled, Manly got the penalty and kicked for touch. Two minutes later, Donnelly had the ball and ran into the defence, with his elbow raised. That elbow clocked his sparring partner Randall and the brawl was on again, with players rushing to join in. Match footage shows Boyd was particularly keen to join in; he rushes to the brawl so fast it's like there's a giant magnet in the middle and he's wearing a jersey made of metal.

The final score would get overshadowed by the biff but Wests would win the game 13-7, placing them in the top five for the first time – and they would remain there for the rest of the season. Only one person would be sent off during this feisty match, but it didn't arise from either brawl. In the second half Manly winger Steven Knight coathangered Wests' Wayne Smith; the centre stepped inside Knight on a break and Knight flung out an arm to stop him, which went high. No Wests players was marched in this game; in fact, despite the team team's reputation for violence, they wouldn't have a single player sent off all season.

For all the folklore built around this Lidcombe clash, the Wests-Manly game wasn't the worst of the round. That same afternoon, St George and Parramatta played at Kogarah Oval. It was the first time the two sides met since the 1977 grand final replay, where Saints had sailed close to wind in terms of physicality and illegality.

So the Eels were keen to return serve. The *Herald*'s Alan Clarkson was at the game. "Tackles were loaded and really meant to hurt. There were punches and two Parramatta players had teeth marks on their stomachs," he wrote. "There were a couple of headbutts and several Parramatta players complained that knuckles had been ground into their eyes."

Three players were marched – Dragons prop Craig Young was the first for kneeing an opponent in the back at the 20-minute mark. Eels players Lew Platz and Ed Sulkowicz were also sent off, the latter after allegedly whacking Saints five-eighth Ken Kearney in the face and opening up a wound over his right eye.

In terms of those biting claims, *The Sun* would report that Eels players John Mann, Lew Platz and Richard Quinn were all bitten, and Graeme Olling also fell victim of the same set of teeth in the reserve grade match.

There was plenty of handwringing coverage about the matches in the days following, with both games getting plenty of space in Sydney's afternoon tabloids. The Lidcombe Oval clash would get more attention – and would be remembered decades later while the more brutal Kogarah clash was forgotten – because it was the TV match of the round. The Lidcombe fisticuffs were screened in suburban lounge rooms that night, causing the league to be most concerned about its good name. And that match footage would very quickly become a problem for Wests.

Masters would claim he didn't tell the players to start a punch-up, though he would have known what the results of his locker-room rev-up would be. And anyway, he said, it's what the public want. "The publicity and the claims of placing the game in disgrace are way off beam," he told *The Sun*'s Peter Peters. "If Wests played Manly tomorrow and the first 20 minutes was promised to be repeated there would be 50,000 to see the match."

For all the brouhaha about the Wests-Manly match, only one of the five players suspended at the league judiciary on Monday played in that game. Manly's Knight got four weeks for the high tackle, the same punishment as Young, Platz and Ted Goodwin from the Kogarah game, with Sulkowicz getting a week off and a $50 fine.

But the league wasn't done with Wests. Using footage of both games, the judiciary cited another five players – three of whom came from the Saints-Eels match. Eels hooker Ron Hilditch was cited for punching, while Rod Reddy and Robert Stone were to come and discuss biting allegations. Hilditch would get a two-week suspension, while it seems nothing further happened to Reddy or Stone.

Donnelly and Boyd were also cited to appear at Wednesday night's special judiciary hearing. Donnelly would be outed for three weeks for punching Randall and his later use of the elbow, while Boyd copped four weeks.

In a further sign the league had had enough of brawling, the referees in those games would also face repercussions. Kogarah referee Gary Cook was relegated to a minor first grade game that weekend – Balmain versus the second-last placed Norths at Leichhardt – while Braybrook was dropped to reserves due to his handling of the Wests-Manly match. They had both also received death threats in the days after what the media briefly tagged Bloody Sunday. The dropping of referees who couldn't control violence in games would lead to the resurrection of the controversial Greg Hartley from reserve grade to the 1978 finals.

While it wasn't the first time the league had cited players on video evidence, the move made Wests officials very unhappy. Club president Bill Carson would accuse the league of bias against his club. "I believe there is a set against Wests at headquarters and I told executive director Ken Humphreys this yesterday," he said to *The Sun*'s EE Christensen. "We have been most harshly treated and only because the game was on TV.

"What happened in our match was nothing [compared] to last year's grand final and grand final replay. Clubs were congratulated by the league after those matches and there was no retrospective viewing of films by the judiciary then."

Masters would also question the fairness of the league's actions, which would feed into the "us against them" mindset he was building at Wests. "I am incensed with the decision handed down tonight," he said after the Wednesday night judiciary hearing. "It is apparent that the rugby league executive committee has already decided on their final five for 1978 and, just as obviously, Western Suburbs are not one of them."

The club would also consider banning TV coverage of its matches, before saner heads prevailed and the move was canned. Later in the season, the club had no issues with the judiciary using video evidence when it worked in Wests' favour. In the last round of the '78 season, Wests played Cronulla and Sharks forward Dane Sorensen would be suspended for four weeks after the league viewed match footage from Channel 7 (the same channel that aired the Wests-Manly match). This meant the Sharks' key forward would miss the finals season that started the following week. And who was Cronulla playing in the first week of the finals? Wests.

Boyd didn't like the four weeks' suspension he copped and, in a move that ran counter to the image he was a brutal footballer lacking in brains, he took the league to court. He claimed he was denied natural justice because, among other gripes, the league did not notify him of the hearing, he was not shown the entirety of the evidence against him and was not allowed to call witnesses.

After a day-long hearing in the NSW Equity Court on Friday, May 20, the judge said he would hand down his decision on the following Wednesday. In the meantime, he ruled that Boyd was free to play in that weekend's match against Souths at Redfern, which he did. Though he couldn't help the team to a win; the match ended in an 11-all draw.

Three days later, the court ruled Boyd's suspension was null and void. Club boss Carson was "delighted" and said the ruling proved the league had problems when it came to citing players on video evidence. Boyd would play again the following weekend, scoring a try in a 26-16 win over North Sydney at Lidcombe.

But the joy would be short-lived; in a move that smacked of vengeance, the league decided to retry Boyd's case. This time they would allow him to call witnesses and whatever else was needed to make the decision legal. Boyd would end up receiving the same sentence – four weeks on the sideline.

Boyd was no stranger to the judiciary; he had been suspended three times in the 1977 season for a total of eight games. After the 1978 ban, he would get a two-week ban for fighting in 1979 and six weeks for treading on an opponent in 1980 (by which time he had switched to Manly). Then came a dark stretch between 1983 and 1985, where he would play just three games.

In June 1983 he was suspended for a year after breaking Daryl Brohman's jaw in a State of Origin match. He returned to first grade on June 16, 1984, but would only play three matches before being cited for eye gouging Bulldogs' Billy Johnstone after the league had reviewed video evidence. Johnstone was called to attend by the judiciary, answering "no comment" to every question about the incident.

Calling gouging "reprehensible" and saying strong action was needed when it was detected, judiciary boss Jim Comans handed Boyd a 15-month suspension. That match against the Bulldogs would be the last time Boyd would play in the NSW rugby league competition.

As for the 1978 Magpies, they would lose the rematch against Manly at Brookvale 16-10. Masters said they had to dial back the aggression to stop referee Hartley from taking action. "We knew there would be a bloke sent off if we growled at them," Masters said. "We are not too confident about our blokes going before the judiciary."

Still, the Magpies finished minor premiers on 33 points – three points clear of Cronulla and Manly in equal second. But the siege mentality that led to them being undefeated at Lidcombe Oval didn't work so well on the open expanses of the Sydney Cricket Ground come finals time. The team that finished on top of the ladder would be bundled out in straight sets. They would go down 14-10 to Cronulla in the major semi and then lose the final to Manly 14-7.

Referee Hartley caused controversy in that finals series; most notably for his poor tackling counts in the minor semi replay between Manly and Parramatta, including one instance where the Sea Eagles scored on the seventh tackle.

Because of the controversy swirling around Hartley – and the belief he was favouring Manly – Wests fans would look to him as the reason they didn't win the premiership in 1978. It's an idea that overlooks the fact Wests lost both of their final matches, though Hartley was only in charge of one.

As evidence players point to a Graeme O'Grady try Hartley disallowed early in the second half of the final, which could have levelled the scores at 10-all. O'Grady kicked the ball and then grounded it over the line, and today several players insisted Hartley disallowed the try because O'Grady was offside. In the excellent documentary *The Fibros and the Silvertails* O'Grady says captain Tom Raudonikis asked Hartley "How can he be offside? He put the ball up".

But the TV footage of that try clearly shows Hartley signaling for a knock-on, and then packing a scrum. If O'Grady had been ruled offside, why did Hartley pack a scrum rather than award Manly a penalty?

In media coverage the next day, Masters himself said it was disallowed for a knock-on – though he disputed that Wests had knocked it on. The claim that a fair try was disallowed because Hartley ruled the kicker was offside just isn't true.

The stats suggest Wests got a fair shake. The penalties were 13-all, the scrums 7-all and the Magpies made fewer tackles than the Sea Eagles, which suggests the men in black had a greater share of the ball.

That said, Hartley was partially responsible for Wests not winning the comp. But that was a result of Wests' own making. They ramped up the brutality in the 1978 season, which forced the league to take action. That included dropping referees who wouldn't take charge of the game, leading directly to Hartley being returned to the top grade. Say what you will about him, the referee could stand up to players. Even Masters acknowledged as much in *The Fibros and the Silvertails*, saying "I think Hartley was better equipped to deal with the violence on the field. We've got to give him that."

He wasn't the best referee overall. Prone to over-the-top displays on the field that seemed designed to catch the camera's eye, he made some eye-watering blunders. Everyone knows about those seven-tackle sets but forgotten is an even more glaring mistake he made a year earlier in an Easts-St George match. In that game he awarded Rooster Bob Fulton a field goal even though he clearly punted the ball through the sticks. While it had no effect on the score, Hartley was dropped to reserve grade for that. And he would be dropped several more times in his career.

Ray Chesterton, author of a history of the Manly Sea Eagles, says Hartley "was always a flawed referee whose technical mastery of the job was questionable at times." While he wasn't the best referee in terms of ability, he was the best referee for the job in 1978 – the job of coming down hard on on-field violence.

<u>1978</u>
Australia Vs A Punk Band

There were some rules about what stories made the cut for *Biff*. For one, they had to be fights; swinging arms, elbows or cheap shots didn't qualify – that's why Les Boyd smashing Daryl Brohman isn't here. Yeah, it was violent, but it wasn't a fight. Another piece of criteria was that they had to had to take place on the field. That meant no dust-ups in the car park after training, or during Mad Monday celebrations.

That second rule had to be broken to include this story, because it was so odd that I couldn't leave it out. It's about the time the Kangaroos fought it out with members of 1970s mod band The Jam. See, it's weird, right?

The incident happened in Leeds on November 13, 1978 (at least one book on The Jam mistakenly places it during the band's tour for the album *This Is The Modern World*, which was released a year earlier) in the team hotel. One version of the story says the team hotel was the Dragonara, another says it was the Queens Hotel – that part's not too important.

The key source for the story is a *Sydney Morning Herald* report (headlined "Kangaroos brawl with punk group") from league journo Alan Clarkson, who said team manager Jim Caldwell was glassed, leaving seven gashes across his face. The manager was shifting a chair, which accidentally bumped a member of The Jam, who were drinking in the hotel. That was enough, it seemed, to warrant someone glassing a 59-year-old man.

That someone is usually reported to be Jam frontman Paul Weller, though Clarkson never names him. The singer would spend a night in jail over the incident only to be acquitted in court – so make up your own mind as to whether he did it or not.

Kangaroos winger Larry Corowa was drinking

with Caldwell at the time and stepped in, only to get whacked in the back of the head. He then ran into the main bar to bring in some of his team-mates and a brawl ensued. According to Weller friend and biographer Paolo Hewitt, The Jam bassist Bruce Foxton stepped in to help even though they were outnumbered. "Say what you like about him," Hewitt remembered Weller as saying, "I'll always remember him doing that." Foxton will probably always remember it too; the league players busted a few of his ribs.

"They went berserk," Foxton said of the Kangaroos. "They went mad. It was really frightening. They were after our blood, literally, and we had to leave about three in the morning and check into another hotel. It fucked the rest of the tour because I had badly bruised ribs."

The band's drummer Rick Buckler was also in the pub and he laid out his version of events in his book *That's Entertainment: My Life in The Jam*. He said the band was in the hotel relaxing after a gig and remembered the Australian players being "more than a little tipsy but in good spirits". The trouble started because the hotel was serving residents through a small hatch and a long queue of people was forming.

"Several of us, including Paul, impatiently stood in line. I was sitting on a sofa at the other end of the lobby when we heard what sounded like a tray of drinks hitting the floor. Somebody had apparently turned around and knocked over Paul's drinks and an altercation had taken place, resulting in what turned out to be one of the management for the rugby [sic] team receiving a cut to his head with a glass."

After a brawl, Buckler said the band scarpered off and hid in their rooms from "these large and well-oiled rugby blokes" until the police advised the band it was in their best interests to leave.

But that might not have been the end of it. In Mark Flanaghan's book *The Invincibles*, hooker Max Krilich says some of the Kangaroos formed a posse of sorts to hunt down The Jam (whom he referred to as "scumbags").

"I was in bed when Allan McMahon and a few of the others knocked on my door and said "quick, get up! We are going to chase a couple of blokes from The Jam'," he said. "I was playing in the midweek game so I stayed in bed but I think they went and gave them a hiding. There wasn't much discussion about it afterwards because the deed had been done."

There you have it – a strange footnote in the history of international rugby league.

1981
Newtown Vs Manly

When a brawl erupts in the first minute or two of a match, it's a pretty safe bet that a bit of planning has gone into it. The players aren't reacting to something that happened on the field, but a decision made in the dressing sheds to put the stink on at a certain time. Maybe it's the first tackle that is the agreed-upon sign, maybe the second scrum, but the players make sure to synchronise their watches so they all know what to expect and when to expect it.

This was surely the case in the Newtown-Manly argy-bargy in the 1981 finals, which is one of the most infamous brawls of all time. Rex Mossop was behind the mic for the Channel 7 coverage, describing it thusly; "That is the most frantic opening to a rugby league match I've seen in 35 years". And he'd have some experience in this field, having been in a few dust-ups in his time.

But just whose idea was it? The inimitable Les Boyd was wearing Manly colours that day and he insisted the Sea Eagles didn't cross the white line looking for blood. "Newtown may have had a plan, but we didn't," he told Roy Masters for his book *Bad Boys*. "We had blokes in our side like Bruce 'Goldie' Walker, and they weren't really fighters. Bowden tells people that I started it with a punch from the second row in a scrum, but Newtown put the blue on."

Tommy Raudonikis was the Jets captain and he said his team didn't head out wanting a fight. "We didn't speak about putting the blue on, but the blue happened because of me and Manly and what we were about."

The likely truth is the blame for the brawl rests with Raudonikis – who is always a prime suspect when it came to fights starting – and Jets prop Steve Bowden. In the lead-up to the game, the tabloids beat up suggestions that Manly's Mark Broadhurst had planned to sort out Bowden. While the Manly prop would always claim he'd been misquoted, Bowden obviously grabbed hold of that slight and used it as motivation. And all the evidence you needed for that was the resulting battered, bruised and swollen face of Broadhurst, which had met Bowden's fists – and skull – a number of times during the brawl.

The brawl tends to overshadow what was a good season for the 1981 Jets, after quite a few lean years in the 1970s. They made the finals in 1973 – the first year of the top five – but would be stopped one game short of the grand final by Cronulla. Things went downhill from there, bottoming out with an embarrassing wooden spoon threepeat in 1976-77-78. In those three seasons they won just seven games out of a total of 66. But long-suffering fans were rewarded with a 1981 season that saw them win 14 games and become embedded in the top five from Round Six. And come September, they started dreaming of their first grand final appearance since 1955 and their first premiership since 1943.

Those dreams began to look shaky right from the

start of the finals series. They lost the major preliminary semi 10-8 to Parramatta, with replacement Ken Wilson shanking a kick from in front late in the game. That put them into an elimination semi against Manly, who had finished in fifth and knocked out Cronulla in the first round of the finals

Some of the boys in blue were keen to knock out Manly – in more ways than one. The early appearances were that Bowden wasn't the only Newtown player gunning for Broadhurst. In just the second tackle, Bowden's front row partner Steve Blyth went in on Broadhurst, who got up swinging. Clearly he resented something Blyth had done in the tackle but as to what that was it's hard to tell on the TV coverage – those chunky onscreen graphic overlays so beloved of 1980s footy coverage obscure whatever happened.

But worse was about to come Broadhurst's way. Manly kicked downfield on the next tackle and Jets fullback Phil Sigsworth spilled the ball. So queue the scrum. *The* scrum, if you're a Jets player.

"Both teams were primed for trouble in the first scrum," the *Herald*'s Alan Clarkson wrote on the Monday after the game. "The Newtown forwards were told that Manly would 'turn it on' in the first scrum. Manly were told that Newtown would be the aggressors. Gocher was told by another referee before the match that Newtown would start the trouble in the first scrum."

Today we're spoilt as TV footy viewers. There are cameras everywhere at the ground; think of an angle you want and there will be a camera that captured it. That wasn't the case in 1981, they had one, maybe two cameras. Which is a problem for what is about to happen.

Manly's half John Gibbs feeds the scrum and its won by the Jets and the camera immediately follows Raudonikis as he runs the ball into the Manly defence. But the action's happening back at the scrum, which has erupted off-camera. That scrum was also the first time in the game Bowden has come into contact with Broadhurst.

What happened in those crucial seconds before the

scrum broke up we'll never really be able to see because Channel 7 didn't have a camera on it at the time. In the few seconds it takes for the camera to pan back, the brawl on, and every member of the scrum (barring the Manly forward who broke early to tackle Raudonikis) is at it.

The camera's focal point is the Bowden-Broadhurst battle, where both players have a handful of jersey and are swinging a huge number of punches with their free hands. Broadhurst already seems to be sporting a shiner while they're both standing toe-to-toe, before the really nasty stuff happens. Bowden headbutts the Manly prop, who then goes weak at the knees. Bowden roughly helps him to the ground before lying on top of him and raining at least five punches straight into the face of a defenceless Broadhurst.

Elsewhere former Wests team-mates Raudonikis and Les Boyd are meeting up, as other players try and break up various brawls, only for others to start.

Somewhere in there, Manly's Terry Randall would do something that would cause him problems with the judiciary. It seems to happen towards the end of the brawl, when he rushes out of a pack of blue jerseys, with his arms over his head to ward off the blows raining down.

Once it all cools down, referee John Gocher calls in Bowden and Randall to give them both their marching orders. Unbelievably, no camera captures this moment, and Mossop nor sideline eye Barry Ross seemed to be paying attention, which prompted this amusing master-servant interchange between the pair.

"Barry, do you know whether it's sinbin or send-off?"

"I didn't see a sinbin ..."

"Well, go and ask ... *please*."

"Yes, I shall."

"Thank you, it's fairly important that we know this."

Mossop missed the ref's call too but somehow thinks it's all Ross' fault. For the record Bowden and Randall were sent off. Though, surprisingly, neither were sent to the showers for fighting; Bowden went for headbutting, while Randall's crime was kicking.

Just three tackles later, Raudonikis would kick it off again when he charged Boyd and then threw away the ball so he could punch the forward. He stayed on the field. In fact, no-one in the entire match would be sent off for punching.

If Raudonikis had brought the Western Suburbs philosophy of brawling early to get their opponent off their game over to Newtown, it worked. Manly – who had scored more points that season than Newtown – looked shaky for the first half. Early in the second half the Jets would take the lead out to 16-nil before Manly would starting putting it all together. They would score 15 points in the last 30 minutes, but it wouldn't be enough to get them through to the following weekend. The Jets would win 20-15 and go onto meet minor premiers Easts in the final.

Despite having two black eyes since the fifth minute Broadhurst would play the entire match. They were so swollen he couldn't see; telling hooker Max Krilich to hand him the ball rather than pass it. After the game he would tell *The Sun* he copped a few punches from the second row in that first scrum.

Referee Gocher had a different view of things. After the match, he would point the finger at Broadhurst for starting the fight. "He threw punches in the scrum which led to the brawl. I didn't send him off because the charge against him was only punching. Probably no one would have been sent off but for the seriousness of the charges against Terry Randall and Steve Bowden."

The afternoon tabloids' back pages feigned outrage over the brawl for days; *The Sun* ran the headline "150 seconds of shame" over an enlarged photo of Bowden delivering a right-handed uppercut. *The Mirror*'s back page demanded "STOP THIS!: SCG carnage", complete with a photo of Bowden laying into a prone Broadhurst.

With the brawl into people's lounge rooms and later replayed in news bulletins on three channels, the league didn't like the way it made them look. That the biff happened wasn't so much the problem; like the 1978 Wests-Manly dust-up, the issue was that loads of people got to see it on the TV broadcast. The league was so unimpressed with the TV networks that, at one stage, it was even looking to take action against them for continuing to show the brawl. Through a deal they'd all signed with the league, the networks had agreed not to show footage that brought "the game into disrepute" (yes, they were using that phrase in 1981) and the league was considering enforcing that.

Ultimately, league boss Kevin Humphreys would let them off with a warning at the Monday night judiciary hearing. "We will inform the television stations that further breaches will not be tolerated," he said. The stations paid him no mind, airing footage of the brawl in their coverage of the judiciary.

Randall would get six weeks on the sideline for kicking Bowden in a melee. In the 1982 season, three weeks after returning to the field from the suspension, he would clean up a Cronulla player in a reserve grade fixture and cop a nine-week suspension. Randall would play just four games in the top grade that season, with that reserve grade incident a factor in his decision to retire at the end of the '82 season.

As for Bowden, well, he was a player not

unfamiliar with the goings-on of the judiciary. He was suspended for two weeks in 1979, sent off and sidelined for two weeks in 1980 and, in the 1981 State of Origin match he would be up to his elbows in two separate fights, turning up to Newtown training the following night with two black eyes.

The judiciary would sit for four hours to hear Bowden's case. Represented by solicitor John Hughes, his defence was that, when he delivered the headbutt, he was concussed from the earlier punches he'd received, calling a psychiatrist and the club doctor in to testify.

It didn't help, judiciary boss Jim Comans would ban Bowden for five weeks, ruling him out of what would be his only chance to play a top-flight grand final. And, one could argue, damaging the Jets chance of winning the big one.

Bowden would be a forlorn figure at the SCG the following week as the Jets beat Easts 15-5 to head to the grand final. "I am very disappointed that I could not be a real part of the win. It was very hard, I can tell you. I kept replaying in my mind what I might have done out there."

A week later he would watch Newtown match it with the Eels until well into the second half, before the Jets began to falter and Parramatta came home with a wet sail to snare their first premiership.

You can't help but wonder if things would have turned out differently if Bowden was on the field providing some defensive starch.

1982
Bob Cooper Vs Illawarra

Of all the dust-ups mentioned in this book, here is by far the worst. It's an incident that curtailed the careers of no fewer than three of the participants. Two of them were taken to hospital, while the third was rubbed out for more than a year.

It happened at Wollongong Showground (still ringed by a dog track at the time) on a Sunday afternoon in June 1982, but had its origins in a Round Four reserve grade match at Lidcombe Oval earlier that year. In that game, Western Suburbs second-rower Bob Cooper was sent off in the first minute after the referee decided he'd used his knees on an Illawarra Steelers player. He was exonerated by the judiciary but it set the stage for a possible get-square when the Magpies headed south for this Round 18 clash.

Cooper wasn't expecting to play in the top grade at Wollongong but was brought up from reserves after second-rower George Moroko pulled out on the Saturday with injury. On the Sunday, Cooper followed his team-mates out to the warm-up field before the game, and he got a hint of what might be coming. "I was delayed and about 50 metres behind [my team-mates] as I walked out," Cooper told former coach Roy Masters in his book *Bad Boys*. "The Illawarra players were coming back from their warm-up and they had a go at me. 'We're going to get you, Cooper. We're waiting for you'."

Cooper took no notice and kept walking to the practice field. The vibes were so bad that even first grade referee Chris Ward felt them. "The word was there was some ill-feeling between the camps," he told *The Mirror* the day after the June rematch. "I heard things might eventuate. I spoke with both captains before the kick-off, telling them I would not tolerate any fisticuffs. They both let me down."

They got into it very, very quickly. A brawl erupted just 90 seconds after the opening kick-off. Wests hooker Arthur Mountier took a tap and passed it to Paul Merlo, who was hit by Steelers player Greg Cook. Cooper swore Cook went in with a raised elbow and so he ran to his team-mate's aid. There seems to be next to no footage of the brawl that I could source, beyond a few seconds that appear in a Steelers documentary put together by Wollongong's WIN Television. These few seconds make for some gruesome viewing.

In the snippet, Cook appears to hit Cooper, who then retaliates before a Magpies team-mate rushes in and grapples with Cook. "I pop out of the action and then I see Cook's head just sitting there," he told Masters. "I go whack and hit Cook's head." In the footage, Cooper then backs away, as Steelers fullback Lee Pomfret comes in from the side and grabs another Wests player. What follows is what makes this the worst incident in *Biff*. Cooper sees Pomfret come into view and leans into a vicious right-hander that hits the unsuspecting Steeler flush in the face.

Cooper's fist seems to take up Pomfret's entire face. Pomfret's legs turn to jelly and he hits the ground in the middle of the melee, as a third Steeler Scott Greenland joins the pack, only to get hit by Cooper as well.

Referee Ward had no doubts about giving Cooper his marching orders and Cook, still lying on the showground turf, was also sent from the field. The referee had decided his elbow started the proceedings. Cook went to hospital with a suspected fractured skull, while Pomfret had a fractured nose and a broken jaw.

The papers reveled in the brawl in the following days. "45 seconds of mayhem," read the heavy black type on the *Mirror*'s back page the next day. "Two jaws broken in just two minutes!" the paper said inside, overstating things just a bit. Next to a photo of a concussed Pomfret with blood streaming from his nose, one *Sun* back page said "We can't take any more bashings". They followed it a day later with "RL star: risk to eyesight", where they said Cook's career could be over. "Specialists have warned me my eyesight is at risk if I receive another knock," Cook said. The Steelers' home town paper *Illawarra Mercury* would go the hardest, using the same picture of a battered Pomfret on the front page under the headline "It's suicide! Bloody brawls killing league". "The violence that erupted at the start of Sunday's match was a disgrace," editor Peter Newell wrote. "One player is in hospital with a fractured cheekbone, a smashed nose and facial fractures at the base of his nose. Another player went to hospital and has to return there today for treatment for a compound fracture of the nose and a broken upper jaw.

"Punch-ups might be great crowdpullers today. But tomorrow they will be the very reason for the code's death rattle."

In front of a packed press gallery on Wednesday night, the judiciary would meet to hear the case against Cooper, with chairman Jim Comans dropping the hammer on the Wests player. He would suspend Cooper for a massive 15 months – and just for the punch he threw at Cook. The far more brutal punch he delivered to Pomfret wasn't even a factor (on hearing the verdict, the Steelers would withdraw a complaint they'd lodged over the Pomfret punch). Comans classed Cooper's involvement as "an utterly despicable act" and said he had taken on the role of "judge, jury and executioner".

"Acts such as these must be obliterated from the game," Comans told Cooper, "and we will obliterate you from the game. You are suspended until the first day of October, 1983."

In an interview the following day with *The Sun*, Cooper did himself no favours by admitting he didn't know how many players he hit in the melee. "I just kept ducking and punching," the 28-year-old said. "If I hadn't thrown a couple of good punches I would have been alright. But I believe if you are going to hit someone you should hit them properly."

That same day he told *The Mirror*'s Ian Hanson that his professional league career was over. "No club will want my services now, I'm too much of a high risk," he said.

Greg Cook, who was promoting the newly-formed Steelers in Wollongong schools as a liaison officer, feared the brawl had wiped away all his good work. "Everything was going along so well until Sunday," he said, "the feeling among the players was terrific and the public were beginning to accept us in the Sydney league.

"I was getting a tremendous response from the schools and kids in the area in my capacity with the club. But that one brawl has done so much damage, I don't think I'll be able to rectify it."

Cook's own appearance before the judiciary would be delayed two weeks and, when he did turn up, Comans exonerated him. "Whatever occurred between Merlo and Cook did not cause the all-in brawl," Comans said. "Player Cooper, who rushed in, took the law into his own hands. There have been accusations that Cook was the cause of what happened. I say Cook did not cause the brawl, but that player Cooper did."

Cooper didn't accept the 15-month ban without a fight. He took his grievance to the NSW Supreme Court, asking for an injunction to stop the ban on him playing. His lawyer Michael Finnane said Cooper had been prepared to plead guilty to fighting but was unaware a charge of delivering an unnecessary and vicious blow would be levelled against him.

He was out of luck – Justice Helsham ruled Cooper had kicked things off. "Cooper had intended to deal with player Cook in a way in which Cooper thought was appropriate," Justice Helsham said. "In my opinion, the commonsense conclusion is that the fight started when he did just that – he started to fight when he took to Cook.

"To say that he was not fighting when he began the whole thing just does not make sense to me."

The Magpies forward served his suspension, playing Australian rules in the Sydney competition. Despite believing his name would be mud with league teams, in 1984 North Sydney signed him to his biggest contract ever; but he would play just four games before he busted his elbow and dislocated his shoulder.

Still, he lasted longer than most of the Steelers players he hit. Cook's top grade career would be over at the end of 1983. As for Pomfret, he would make it back and play 15 games in the 1983 season. But that would be his last year in the top grade as well.

It would be the last Steeler hit, Scott Greenland, whose post-brawl playing career would be the longest. He'd be with the Steelers until the end of the 1986 season, playing a total of 44 matches for the fledgling club.

<u>1984</u>
NSW Vs Queensland

The Sydney footy media indulging in a bout of hand-wringing after NSW losses in State of Origin matches may seem like something new, but it's been going on almost since the series' inception. In 1980 and 1981, the Origin concept was tested in what would have otherwise been a dead rubber after NSW won the first two games in each of those years. By 1982, the powers that be finally realised this Origin thing could be a goer, and so the first three-game Origin series was played in 1982.

Just a year later, after Queensland won the first match of the 1984 series *Sydney Morning Herald* journalist Phil Derriman went a bit overboard. "NSW's loss to Queensland in their rugby league match on Tuesday night provided further evidence, if it were needed, that this once proud state is a spent force in Australian sport."

In that 1984 series, it's not Game One that most people remember, it's the second one – at the Sydney Cricket Ground. The one where NSW must have thought, 'if we can't win the game, at least we can win the fight'. You would never hear of it these days but in the lead-up to the Tuesday night match, senior figures in NSW rugby league gave the green light for a punch-up. In *The Mirror* Jack Gibson quoted judiciary chairman Jim Comans' comments a few days earlier, where he said it'd be alright with him if players hit each other. "If two players roll around and throw a few punches, no damage is done and the crowd gets its money's worth," Comans said. "I think the crowd enjoy the hit-ups."

Gibson was so stunned he contacted Comans to confirm the report was correct. It was. League boss John Quayle agreed with the sentiment, stating that "punch-ups are a part of the game".

The supercoach saw the writing on the wall, and

made this prediction on the day of the second match. "With tonight's State of Origin and the coming Test match between Great Britain, we can now virtually assure the customers that a brawl will eventuate," Gibson wrote.

He was right on both counts. The Test saw the forward packs trade blows on two occasions – though the referee must have thought fighting *wasn't* part of the game as he binned the participants. As for that State of Origin match on June 20, 1984, Gibson's prediction came true after just two tackles.

That game had a referee more amenable to the league's desire to see forwards whack each other in the face. Queenslander Barry Gomersall was a controversial and confusing figure – especially to NSW fans, who were convinced he was biased towards the Maroons. This was obviously untrue, as the incident where Les Boyd broke Daryl Brohman's jaw in the first game of the '83 Origin series shows. Everyone remembers that moment, but few remember that Gomersall (who was the ref that night) let Boyd stay on the field. Don't you think a pro-

Maroons ref would have given Boyd his marching orders for that? Of course you do. Boyd only ended up with his one-year ban after Brohman's club Penrith lodged a complaint.

In terms of 1984's Game One and its impending biff, Gomersall was the right man to see it grow. He took the view that if players wanted to fight, he'd leave them to go at it while he got on with the match. And he stuck to that view too. In a National Panasonic Cup match between a Combined Brisbane side and South Sydney at Lang Park a month earlier, he ignored what was virtually an all-in brawl. Just four players chose to keep playing football rather than get involved. "In that National Panasonic Cup I was lucky, because play could continue," Gomersall told the *Sun-Herald*. "And South Sydney was unfortunate because two rucks later one of them knocked on when there were two South Sydney players against bugger-all Brisbane defence and they could have scored … and it would have stood."

But there was no doubt the real estate agent from Mackay was dedicated to his refereeing job. He would spend a lot of his time during the footy season crisscrossing Queensland to officiate games at all levels. On the weekend before 1984's Game One, the Grasshopper had reffed in his hometown junior matches on Saturday, before driving 80 kilometres for a senior match. Come Sunday, he clocked up a 700-kilometre round trip to be the man in the middle for the Great Britain-North Queensland match in Townsville.

And here he was in Sydney to tackle a State of Origin match that had been primed for a punch-up. Gomersall knew something was going to happen; before the game, the touch judges went into the sheds to check on each team and told the ref how wound up both sides were.

When talking about this game, it's become a cliché to say the on-field fireworks kicked off before the smoke had cleared from the actual fireworks lit off the field. And it's true; whoever was in charge of the pre-match entertainment got the timing wrong. With rain pouring from the skies, the fireworks start seconds before Ross Conlon kicks off the brown-

and-white striped ball and they're booming as Queensland fullback Colin Scott picks it up in his in-goal and carries it out to get tackled around eight metres upfield.

He plays the ball back to hooker Greg Conescu, who has the plan to fling it back to Gene Miles to roost it downfield. NSW half Steve Mortimer jumps out from second marker and pressures big Geno, stopping the kick. Then three forwards – Steve Roach, Peter Tunks and Origin debutante Royce Simmons – gang-tackle Miles, with Roach appearing to swing a fist at his head and a second to the ribcage.

Gomersall sees it and immediately cocks his arm and awards Queensland a penalty. But absolutely no one is paying any attention. Even as the Grasshopper's hand goes up, so do those of Queensland forward Greg Dowling, right into Roach's head. From there everyone gets involved and there is so much going the TV cameras keep switching angles trying to cover it all. Look over there, Queensland centre Chris Close is pushing past a few team-mates to have a go at NSW lock Ray Price. Then there's another camera shot showing Paul Vautin wandering around in the background looking for a fight to join. In the foreground is Roach lying on top of Conescu, whose legs are spread. It all looks quite odd, like there's loving, not fighting, going on there.

So we jump back to Close and Price, and the latter's Eels team-mate Brett Kenny has arrived to hold Close down so Price can stand and use gravity to help rain down a few more blows. Now we get a wide shot showing two separate tussles going on – in all this Miles still has the ball in his hands – and a third sparking up involving Close (whose jersey has largely been yanked off and only covering his left arm).

Another camera angle and there's Close – who really is in the thick of things – seemingly kneeing a bent-over Blues player in the face. Tunks doesn't like that so he has a go at Close; a few haymakers ensue before Tunks bends forward and Close delivers a right-handed uppercut or two after which the pair suddenly stop, followed by the rest of the players, as though their angry juice has all run out.

Gomersall calls out Mortimer, Price and Roach for

a chat. Close lingers behind the referee and touch judges as if he figures his turn will come next. But then a load of other players of both teams mill about as it becomes clear Gomersall is delivering one great big caution to all 26 players (oh for a miked-up referee). Then he returns to the spot where he originally awarded the Queensland penalty before the 37-second brawl started – yeah, it was just 37 seconds but it seems a whole lot longer than that.

Some would later have a little go here and there. Roach would have a go at Miles in a tackle, but give away a penalty. Dowling would later retaliate, getting away with punching Roach in the face in full view of Gomersall.

The final winner would be Queensland, who managed to handle the feisty, muddy conditions better than NSW and come away with a 14-2 win. A highlight was Dowling somehow managing to catch a wet footy centimetres off the muck of the SCG surface, keep control of it and dive over for a try.

As for the brawl, Gomersall would shrug it off. "There's nothing you can do in those situations," he would say after the game. "But once they got it off their chests it was a bit of a relief and I knew I had the match."

It certainly didn't do his chances of selection any harm – he'd referee in the next four Origin series and some World Cup fixtures.

<u>1984</u>
St George Vs South Sydney

Once upon a time, before the league discovered the existence of points differential and how they could be used to rank teams, top sides finishing the season on the same points had to submit to a playoff game before they were allowed into the finals.

That was the fate that befell the 1984 South Sydney Rabbitohs, who won their last game to finish equal fifth with the Raiders on 30 points. Under today's system, the Bunnies would have gotten in anyway, because their for and against was better than the that of the Raiders. But it was the olden days, so both sides had to turn up to the Sydney Cricket Ground two days after the end of Round 26 to play a sudden death playoff. The Raiders shouldn't have bothered making the trip down to the big smoke; they got walloped in more ways than one. The scoreboard read 23-4 in the Bunnies' favour and the players got involved in an all-in brawl early in the first half.

The win would set up another sudden death match, the minor preliminary semi against Manly just four days later. The extra game looked to have exhausted the Bunnies, who watched as Manly shot out to a 14-0 lead in the first 15 minutes. The score was unchanged at half-time, but something happened in the sheds; Souths came out and scored 22 points to Manly's four to win 22-18. And without any fisticuffs.

That lack of fisticuffs would change – and in a big way – the following week when they met the Roy Masters-coached St George. The Dragons had given up a 16-10 lead against the Eels the week before to fall 22-16, which relegated them to the knockout minor semi.

And Souths were keen to take the idea of a "knockout" match to heart. As Masters would later tell it, he'd heard the Bunnies planned to put on a stink at the second scrum (because doing it at the first would be too obvious). He would go so far as to tip the refs off in the media, suggesting they appoint someone "who can control violence" and citing the all-in brawl between the two teams in the Charity Shield earlier that year.

Dragons prop Craig Young was also gearing up for some fisticuffs. "There is no way we'll start the biff," he told *The Mirror*, "but if Souths want to put it on then we'll gladly accommodate them."

On game day, Steve Rogers would take the field as captain, having played reserve grade the week before on his way back from injury. He may have put the jinx on the Dragons' grand final hopes a few days earlier when he told the papers, "this is my big chance, the chance to captain a premiership-winning side". When it comes to the finals, Dragons fans know you don't get ahead of yourself like that.

Rogers would kick off and it wouldn't take long for Souths' intentions to surface. After a few tackles, Souths Neil Baker kicked downfield. Dragons fullback Brian Johnson gathered the ball and was tackled, only to have Souths centre Darren McCarthy wind up and telegraph the most overt swinging arm you will ever see in your life. The touch judge was right there on the sideline, but he could have been in the back row of the grandstand and still called it.

After a minute and 50 seconds, Dragons half Perry Haddock kicks into touch and the first scrum packs. As promised, no fisticuffs ensue. About two minutes later it's a different story, when Souths forward Billy Hardy tries to bite off too many metres and puts his kick out on the full. The Dragons have the scrum in great attacking position, inside Souths' quarter. St George wins the scrum, lock Graeme O'Grady breaking early to form an extra man in the backline. He takes the pass from Haddock and then offloads to Rogers, who darts across field before he is tackled. But it's obvious something is happening in the scrum, which is now out of the camera shot.

When Rogers is tackled, a few Bunnies players leave the defensive line – even though the Dragons are less than 10 metres from the line and referee Barry Barnes is playing on – and head off camera towards the scrum.

The Dragons have the advantage in terms of numbers, and the remaining Souths players know it. When Johnson is tackled short of the line, two South players lie on him and try to stop him from rising to his feet. When one is lifted off by a rival, Darren McCarthy comes in and literally lies on top of the Dragons fullback, because if he gets up and plays the ball, the Dragons will score. So that starts a bit of biff on the left hand side of the field, but the pause in the run of play gives the camera (it seems the TV network only had one at the ground) the chance to go back to the still seething brawl on the other side.

And pretty much everyone is at it. Even Slippery Steve Morris, one of the tiniest men on the field has a go, lunging at Souths half Craig Coleman. O'Grady and Fenech take it over the sideline and into the advertising hoardings. Pretty much all the players follow, including captain Rogers, who goes after Hardy like he wants to inflict some pain. Just about the only player not involved is Johnson; the camera shows him walking between several of the brawls and just looking at them.

At one stage commentator Ray Warren announces "they're still fighting and the crowd is booing". But they weren't showing their disapproval of the fight. Many were choosing to follow the action on the big screen that made up part of the scoreboard and they weren't impressed when someone in the league hierarchy ordered the pictures be turned off.

Throughout the melee Barnes and his touch judges are seen urging the players to stop. They eventually did, though more likely because they're buggered than anything the officials were saying. Barnes cautions several Souths players, as well as Dragons captain Rogers (who apparently said rude words to a touch judge) but in a brawl that involved pretty much every player on the field, he couldn't find anyone to send off.

The league would later have a similar problem (by the way, the Dragons won the match 24-6 after overcoming a 6-4 half-time deficit). League boss John Quayle came out in Monday's papers, saying the league took a dim view of the goings-on. "Members of the board have expressed concern over the brawl and the board will receive a full report this week," he said. There was even a suggestion that teams could be fined $2000 each. But in the end, well, nothing happened. An all-in brawl and no-one was suspended, no-one was even fined. They just got told they were very naughty boys. "The board was satisfied the players from the South Sydney club were the instigators of the conduct," said the board, referring to itself in the third person. "The board was concerned that the St George players who were not involved in the original incident subsequently took part.

"The board condemns the actions of the players of both clubs and decided that the clubs should be severely reprimanded."

Ah yes, nothing as useless as a "severe reprimand" when it comes to stamping out bad behaviour. Sure, they warned all clubs that the next team to do something like this would cop an automatic $5000 fine. But no club took that seriously, not when the league had failed to take action on a brawl that had only just happened.

Running as a background story to the St George-Souths game were reports that Masters' walkie-talkie communications from the grandstand to the sideline were being intercepted in the match against the Eels a week earlier. A report in the *Sydney Morning Herald* said the rival teams' walkie talkies were tuned to the same frequency and so could hear each other. Parramatta officials certainly passed anything important they heard onto Eels coach John Monie. As an example, the *Herald* report stated (the reporter was apparently sitting on the Parramatta bench), when they heard Masters say Graeme Wynn only had five minutes left on the field, Monie was told the Dragons forward was about to be replaced.

To avoid it happening again, Masters switched to a marine frequency for the Souths match. But he claimed in a later *Sun* column that it didn't work; his messages were intercepted again. "Our equipment man went up to the secretary of one of our opponents and said, 'How do you do it?' 'Oh, we've got a scrambler,' he boasted. 'There's not a frequency you can use that we can't pick up'."

So he took it a step further when the Dragons and Eels met again in the final. He had the SCG Trust install a telephone line down to the bench. It didn't help the Dragons, who would go down 8-7 to the Eels.

1991
Garry Jack vs Ian Roberts

What happens on the field stays on the field, they say. No matter what an opponent dishes out, you're supposed to cop it sweet and not do anything about it once you leave the field return to the real world. Yet this oft-stated belief (usually stated by ex-players who did a fair bit of the dishing-out) hasn't stopped players from pursuing more justice than they got from the referee's whistle.

Sometimes, they take their grievance to court. Perhaps the most well-known case comes from the 1983 Origin match where NSW's Les Boyd breaks Queensland debutante Daryl Brohman's jaw. Boyd would be suspended for 12 months. Brohman, who missed out on Test selection because of the injury, took Boyd to court. A confidential out-of-court settlement was reached, reportedly in the neighbourhood of $35,000; which equates to well over $100,000 in today's money.

Other players have been taken to court for things they did on the field. Steve Rogers sued Canterbury's Mark Bugden after a tackle from the Dogs hooker broke his jaw nine minutes into the first-round match in 1985. Bugden got a 12-week suspension for that and Rogers took him to court five years later. During testimony, Rogers told the court that, after the broken jaw, kissing his wife was "not as enjoyable as it used to be". The court ruled in Rogers' favour, ordering Bugden and the Bulldogs to cough up $69,000.

Both players appealed; Bugden because he disagreed with the original ruling and Rogers because the payout wasn't big enough. Bugden lost while Rogers got an extra $15,000 which included $8000 to compensate for the fact the Sharks star "will have many years to contemplate that he was thrown from the pinnacle of rugby league eminence in those circumstances", Justice Giles ruled.

Dale Shearer was playing for Manly in 1988, when

he was hit in a late tackle by Easts winger David French. The fullback suffered a double fracture of the jaw, and French was suspended for three months. In 1996, Shearer sued French for $100,000, a figure his lawyer said included lost earnings from club (he had signed a contract to play for Widnes in the UK) and rep games.

Watching video of the incident, French agreed the blow was "sickening" but insisted he had no intent to harm Shearer. "I just raised my arm as a reflex action to protect myself," he told the court. The court would rule in Shearer's favour, awarding him $60,000 plus costs.

In 1992, Canterbury's Steve Mortimer was hit with legal action from Cronulla half Mark Wakefield over a 1986 tackle gone wrong that left Wakefield with neck injuries and a concussion. The pair would settle out of court for what was rumoured to be a five-figure sum.

In 1997 Tigers centre Ian McCann won more than $75,000 after taking Mario Fenech and the North Sydney Bears to court over a tackle in May 1992 that left him with 78 stitches in his mouth and jaw.

There's just one court case that I'm aware of that arose out of an on-field brawl; a battle between Garry Jack and Ian Roberts. In 1991, the Balmain Tigers were in the first of three seasons with Alan Jones as coach (for the record – and because Jones himself is unlikely to ever say so – he didn't do much good. Jones' Tigers won 24 and lost 39 games over that period with a highest-placed finish of 10th). Round 13 saw them playing Manly at Leichhardt Oval and they managed to surprise everyone by racking up a convincing 24-8 win.

An incident just after the half-time siren would have a ripple effect that would go on for eight years. Balmain half Brian Smith put up a bomb and Manly fullback Matthew Ridge was barrelled as he took it, with the whistle blown for half-time as soon as Jack and team-mate Tim Brasher tackled him. Footage of the incident is limited; a snippet that featured as part of a TV news story at the time shows some of what happened. After referee Graeme West blew his whistle for half-time, Jack and team-mate Tim

Brasher kept driving Ridge and another Manly player back towards the tryline. Jack leapt into the air, right arm cocked as if to punch Ridge, who was on the other side of the group. Any potential punch was rendered impotent as Ridge managed to pull himself out of the melee.

Just as Ridge stepped away, a Manly centre swooped in and grabbed Jack's jersey, pulling him out of the huddle. And right on the centre's heel was the towering form of Roberts. He also got a fistful of Jack's jersey before briefly losing his balance and falling to his knees. As he regained his feet, he appeared to use the upward momentum to launch the first in a series of right-hand uppercuts as his left arm rested across Jack's back, holding him in place. In the following days media reports would show Jack's battered face – he'd be left with a pair of swollen eyes and stitches above one and below the other. A week later, he'd find himself in hospital when those cuts became infected, putting his eye-sight in danger.

On the field, both Jack and Roberts received the same penalty – 10 in the bin. The league's response would be put under microscope when it rejected a formal complaint lodged by Balmain. "I received eight uppercuts and it was allowed to pass," Jack told the *Sydney Morning Herald* while also acknowledging he threw the first punch, at Ridge.

The league's inaction on the issue came just weeks after its poor handling of an incident in a State of Origin match where Michael O'Connor had his nose broken in a tackle involving Mal Meninga. Unable to believe no-one was going to take any action, O'Connor himself complained to the NSW Rugby League, who were boxed into a corner and had to cite the Queenslander. However, O'Connor withdrew the complaint after Meninga rang and apologised.

NSWRL general manager John Quayle – who had the only say on which cases were passed onto the judiciary – said the league's view was that the referee had taken action and there would be nothing more done; to refer it to the judiciary would be undermining the on-field official. "In this instance, I believe the referee, in consultation with his touch judges, made the correct decision," Quayle said.

Coaching legend Jack Gibson, himself no fan of league officials, weighed in. He suggested it was not right for O'Connor or Jack to "shriek and squeal" in an attempt to spur the league into action.

When it became clear the league wasn't going to do anything, Jack had solicitor Chris Murphy file a $100,000 lawsuit against Roberts. If the initial brawl and the sight of Jack's injuries was a bad look for the league, it was made worse by the fact their inaction had forced a player into a very public legal fight.

Jack was not unfamiliar with footy incidents turning up in court. Four years earlier, in eerily similar circumstances Eastern Suburbs lodged a complaint against Jack over an alleged late tackle on forward John Mackay that saw him stretchered off with a dislocated hip. Jack received nothing more than a caution from referee Kevin Roberts. Quayle watched the video and decided no further action was warranted. A year later, Mackay took Jack to court seeking $10,000. Jack would settle out of court in 1996.

Jack's case against Roberts would take some time

to find its way before a judge. A hearing would not start until February 1999. Jack would tell the judge the 1991 incident had been an ongoing source of humiliation and embarrassment. "Every day I get people into the store [his Burwood sports store] who saw the incident and remind me of it," he said. "They say, 'didn't you get bashed up by Ian Roberts?'." He said some people would go so far as to shadow box in front of him.

Jack claimed the fight started when Ridge gave him "a jolt under the chin", and Jack tried to hit him, but missed. "Almost instantaneously Ian Roberts came in … and grabbed me with his left arm and there were these punches coming in my face, repeated punches," Jack said.

"I didn't know what had hit me. He was using his right arm to throw uppercuts at me. Roberts had me locked in so there was no chance of me getting away.

"They were the most painful punches I have ever received to the head and face in my 15-year career. I was in a state of shock – it was like being hit with a hammer."

Roberts' team-mate – and Jack's initial target Matthew Ridge would also take the stand. It'd be fair to say the two fullbacks hated each other; Jack had considered taking legal action the previous year over Ridge's autobiography *Take No Prisoners*. He was particularly unimpressed with Ridge describing him as a "dirty bastard" and said "he takes a lot of cheap shots … and if there's a fight, he's off." A few months later, when Ridge would be suspended for eight weeks for eye-gouging, Jack would call for 20 weeks – "The game is certainly better off without him," Jack would say. "If he couldn't kick goals he wouldn't be in any team … he's not what I'd call an attacking fullback."

In the court, passages from Ridge's book were read out, where he described the fight as "ugly". "Garry Jack's a mess, he looks like he's just been beaten up by a gang. He ends up having stitches in his face … it is unbelievable," Ridge had written.

In court, Ridge suggested his ghost-writer was just trying to make the fight seem more interesting. The Manly fullback suggested it was a failed business venture – the particular business remained unnamed – that may have been the reason for the ferocity of Roberts' attack.

The Manly forward was expected to give evidence on the trial's third day but he would never take the stand; Roberts decided to settle for an undisclosed sum. His comments outside the court suggest the settlement was driven by a desire to be rid of the whole thing. "It's been quite an emotional strain, I really didn't realise the stress involved. This has been a thorn in my side for 12 months – I would really love to comment but I just can't." But he would insist that settling the case was "never an admission of guilt".

Days later, the anger would still be there when Jack accused Roberts of ducking out of the court rather than shaking hands. "What a load of crap," Roberts told the *Sun-Herald*. "That sort of talk makes me sick to the stomach. That is pure bullshit.

"As far as I'm concerned, anything I had to pay him was too much. If he wanted to end things on a friendly note why have we had this whole case going on for the past eight years?"

There would be a persistent rumour that Roberts unloaded on the field because Jack had called him a poof. Jack denied that and Roberts would agree; "he didn't say that [but] I can't be bothered going through the whole gay issue again, it will stir a hornets' nest."

In 2016, Roberts would admit that, in a way, it was "the gay issue" that played a role in the punch-up. But it wasn't any issue of Jack's, it was what Roberts was dealing with at the time. He was stuck in a strange middle ground when it came to his sexuality. He was never in the closet while playing – team-mates and opponents knew about it and, judging by the things yelled by the less intelligent members of the crowd, the fans did too. But he was never entirely out of it either; it was a time where a person couldn't just be gay, they had to make some sort of official announcement to the world about it (which is fundamentally unfair – ever heard of a player releasing a statement that he's straight?). While everyone seemed to know, for Roberts, making that announcement seemed a step too far.

It was his struggles to deal with all of this that fed

into the brawl with Jack. "It wouldn't have bothered me then – and I don't say this with any pride – if I'd have killed someone on the field," he said. "I've apologised to Garry and I've spoken to Garry since that. He bore the brunt of my frustration."

1996
Stanley the Steel Avenger vs Balmain

I love it when a mascot misbehaves or becomes a victim of misfortune. And there have been a fair few such incidents scattered through rugby league's history. In 1995, the Red Rooster mascot was at the WACA for the first game of the Western Reds. For reasons that have been lost in the mists of time, he ended up set upon by a large group of children and had to be rescued by none other than the Paddle Pop Lion.

One year the Penrith Panther found himself in a bit of hot water after a Dragons game when St George officials seriously considered citing him for trying to distract their goalkicker. In 2002, the Cowboys had a plethora of mascots, none so bizarre as a giant smiling piece of bread. Nothing happened to him – I just mention it because I'm *still* trying to get my head around that one.

In the Steelers' final seasons, they swapped the beloved Stanley the Steel Avenger for a musclebound goon in a tank top and carrying an inflatable plastic hammer – the odious Sledge. For a guy with heaps of muscles, he was such a sook. In a 1998 home game against the Broncos, he snuck onto the field before kick-off and began tapping the Brisbane players over the head with the hammer. John Plath didn't appreciate that stupidity at all and moved towards Sledge with his fists clenched. Sledge then hightailed it to the sideline.

At a Dragons-Sharks match in 2002, the Happy Dragon became the Cranky Dragon in an altercation with a camera crew. They remonstrated with the Dragon after he stepped on their camera cables. Things escalated and the Happy Dragon allegedly headbutted a crew member. That's right – *headbutted*. To this day I imagine it left the Happy Dragon with a very dented snout.

The baddest mascot of all time must be the Bear

from North Sydney. In a 1994 match at North Sydney Oval against Penrith, the bear swore at touch judge Col Wright. Field operations chief Eric Cox heard of the abuse and ordered him from the field at half-time; though not before ordering the mascot's head be removed so he could ascertain the identity of the swearer inside. The wearer of the Bear suit reportedly copped a three-week suspension from the judiciary.

To the best of my knowledge, only one mascot has been sent off for getting involved in a brawl. That would be Stanley the Steel Avenger – the man in scarlet with a cape and sporting a motorcycle helmet. As the 1995 regular season neared the end, it was a dark time. There was uncertainty in the game with the possible start of the Super League competition the following year. Into that sad time stepped Stanley, who brought a bit of mascot misbehaviour to brighten up the day.

The Steelers were playing Balmain at their beachside home ground in Wollongong. And they were killing the hapless Tigers – the score would end up 32-6. Despite the big win, the game has gone down in league history for what Stanley did in the final minutes of the match. Steelers fullback Brendan O'Meara and Tigers' Mark O'Neill got involved in a bit of a tussle near the sideline. It escalated to involve several other players and ended up continuing over the white stripe – right in front of Stanley the Steel Avenger. The scarlet-clad mascot couldn't help but get involved, though it seems he was trying to break things up.

Referee Tony Maksoud didn't care and pointed Stanley to the sheds. "I ordered him to get off the field," he explained later. "He was right in the thick of it pulling players away. You can't have him man-handling players like that.

"It was nothing that serious, he was just pulling players off but you cannot have him touching the player under any circumstances. He has been mentioned in my report."

O'Meara and O'Neill each got 10 in the bin and the Steelers fullback couldn't believe what had happened to their mascot. "There were punches being thrown left, right and centre and a few players were into it," O'Meara told the *Illawarra Mercury*. "I got pulled off one bloke [O'Neill] and then I looked down and [Stanley] was on the deck. It was unbelievable. Then the ref just said 'you're off'. Stanley was shattered."

The guy inside the suit was a fill-in and the press were eager to talk to the replacement after the match. Steelers CEO Bob Millward pointed out he had already been spirited away from WIN Stadium. "We do not want to reveal the name of the person because we feel he has been embarrassed enough by this whole thing."

After an apology from the club, Stanley the Steel Avenger would escape a suspension and be able to return for the last home game of the season two weeks later against Western Suburbs. "I know how easy it is to become emotional and over-exuberant," said ARL boss John Quayle. "And, goodness me, the game right now is in need of some fun."

Just days before that final home game, the man who was in the suit for that match against the Tigers would reveal himself. He was truck driver Bob

Mitchell, who had donned the costume as a favour to help out a friend who usually wore it on game days.

"One of the Steelers players and a Balmain player, they were fighting and I was on the sideline and what happened was they rolled over towards me and I just put a hand out to pull them apart, which you're not allowed to do – and that's how I came to be sent off," he would tell the *Mercury* several years later.

Two years after the brawl, Stanley the Steel Avenger's days would come to an end. In a misguided attempt to make the Steelers seem more professional and avoid a merger or axing as part of the post-Super League rationalisation, the club introduced the aforementioned Sledge.

The move failed and the club merged with St George the following year. Steelers fans rightly felt sad about the loss of their team – but no-one shed a tear for the disappearance of Sledge.

<u>2003</u>
Gorden Tallis vs Ben Ross

Once tagged the Raging Bull, by 2003, Gorden Tallis was the ageing bull. He'd made his first grade debut with the Dragons back in 1992 and would turn 30 during the 2003 season. Even allowing for the year during the Super League stoush where he sat out the last year of his Dragons contract, 2003 saw him starting his 11th season in the top grade. Add in the State of Origin and Test matches and Tallis' body had played a lot of footy in a decade.

And his body was letting him know about it. Injuries started to see him miss chunks of the season, Between rounds 12 and 26 in the 2003 season, he would play just five games and retire from rep footy at the end of the season. The following season, 2004, would be his last.

But even before the 2003 season kicked off, Tallis could feel himself getting old, could see the writing on the wall. His solution? He would have to punch someone.

He felt rival forwards could see he was fading and would start to give him stick on the field. He believed he had to do something to show he wasn't to be trifled with. So he had a chat with Broncos coach Wayne Bennett and told Benny "I might have to clip a bloke this year".

"What?" the coach replied.

"I might have to fight a bloke," Tallis responded as though it made all the sense in the world.

"Why is that?"

"Because they're all starting to put a bit of shit on me and I don't like it."

The coach said okay, on two conditions; do it early in the season and make sure it was a big guy. No clobbering little halfbacks.

Tallis wouldn't need a long time to find a target; for a big man he had a very thin skin. Witness the 1997 World Club Challenge where he spear-tackled Wigan Warriors forward Terry O'Connor. The Wigan forward gets up and gives Tallis a shove after the play the ball (a thoroughly restrained response after being dumped on your head I would have thought). But Tallis has an enormous over-reaction and immediately starts swinging, landing three punches to O'Connor's face before the Warrior knows what's happening, and at least another four afterwards.

After that fight, Tallis was sent to the sinbin with a smashed-up bloody nose while O'Connor's face came off largely unscathed, suggesting that the Bronco's punches really weren't that powerful.

Compare this to the legendary Mexican stand-off with Terry Hill during State of Origin in 1999. Hill gets up and pushes Tallis – who is at marker – and is immediately ready to go and gets right in the Maroon forward's face. What does Tallis do? He doesn't throw a punch. These incidents and the one we're about to look at from 2003 suggest Tallis prefers the element of surprise when it comes to getting his punches in.

In 2003, Tallis waited all of 59 minutes in the first game of the season before "sending a message". The Broncos were playing away at Penrith. It had rained before the game but the sun had come out, creating a humid stinker of a day. The heat was taking a toll on the players; sweat dripped down their faces and saturated their synthetic jerseys. The Broncos had been handling the heat better than the home side, being up 20-8 at halftime. Eight minutes into the second half, they would extend that lead to 24-8. So by the 59th minute, the Broncos have the game well under control.

Yet this is where Tallis decides to do something that worked for him, but not for the team. Ross, who was playing his first game for the Panthers after leaving the Dragons, was giving it to Tallis – who admitted he was giving it back.

Tallis had started the season with a premeditated plan to punch someone and was just looking for an excuse. And Ross gave it to him when he put his hand on Tallis' throat after tackling him to the ground (though it's clear on the video that Tallis says something to Ross first).

Tallis gets up and gives Ross a shove in the face and then Ross pushes back and then turns his attention to dummy half Richard Swain who has picked up the ball and gone for a run. Tallis isn't at all interested in where the ball was and instead chases after Ross, grabbing a handful of jersey. Perhaps hearing the call of referee Paul Simpkins, Ross turns to him, raising his arms in the air in the recognised footy gesture "hey, I'm not doing anything, it's all the other guy".

Tallis wasn't going to let Ross get away; he'd found the big guy the coach said he could punch. "I said, 'hey mate we're gonna fight'," Tallis would claim years later. "'Whether you like it or not we're going to fight so as soon as you through a punch I'm throwing one back'."

It's a statement that overlooks the fact Tallis threw the first punch – just a second after Ross has turned back from the referee to face him and is therefore unprepared. And then he throws the second. And the third. And the fourth. In fact, on the video it seems he throws at least that many before Ross maybe gets one away. And Tallis then flings out another half dozen before the fight is broken up.

Not surprisingly, Tallis gets 10 in the bin. Surprisingly, so does Ross despite it being clear he tried to walk away and the presence of doubt as to whether he threw any punches at all. As Tallis walked into the sheds, Penrith fans would douse him with orange juice and beer.

While all the attention since the game has focused on the fight, it's worthwhile to note what happens next – the Panthers almost win.

With the Broncos up 24-8, the game looked done and dusted when Tallis left at the 59th minute. Yet, in the first set of six from the penalty on halfway, Luke Priddis scores and Preston Campbell converts – scoreline 24-14. From the kick-off, the Panthers go the length of the field and almost score again. In the 68th minute, with Tallis and Ross still off the field, Luke Lewis would score for the Panthers. With the conversion the score became 24-20 with 11 minutes left.

When Tallis left, his team were 16 points up and when he returned they had just a four-point lead against an opponent suddenly running downhill. Penrith were pushing for the winning try while the Broncos were just hanging on. And the Broncos managed to hang on long enough to rack up the win. A win their captain's selfish actions nearly screwed up for them.

Surprisingly, Tallis wouldn't serve any suspension. NRL spokesman John Brady said the sinbin had been sufficient punishment.

"In this instance it has sailed close to the wind and the commission's decided it wasn't worth a charge," Brady said. "It was two players having a fight, it wasn't everyone coming in and joining in. It wasn't a cheap-shot style of thing."

Ross would disagree with that, labelling Tallis' punches as "cheap shots" straight after the game. "We got told to walk away and next thing I turned away and a cheap shot crashed into my cheek," Ross said. "I've got four stitches and a scar to match the one on the other cheek.

"I'm just disappointed I got sent for 10 because I was just defending myself. I just hate the way representative players get treated a bit differently."

NRL boss David Gallop was of a similar mind, expressing his displeasure to Commissioner Jim Hall that no charges were laid. Gallop had words to Hall and sent the message to players that there would be tougher consequences should this sort of thing happen again.

"We have an independent judiciary and it is not the job of the administration or the board to interfere with individual cases," Gallop said, "but the board can set a clear direction on the standards it would like to see upheld. I made my disappointment known to Jim Hall before the meeting and the views of the board have also been passed on."

The flow-on from the Tallis incident could be seen as the first real sign of the league bosses realising the black eye punch-ups gave the game. While they might appease a segment of those who were already fans, men punching each other in the face didn't do a whole lot to attract new fans. The AFL knew this; their CEO Wayne Jackson saw the Tallis-Ross fight as "the perfect advertisement for Australian rules" because it would turn parents off letting their kids play league.

He felt parents wouldn't want their kids taking part in a sport that saw a punch-up as nothing to worry about. "I reckon I've taken a bit on the field during my lifetime, but I don't want my son or daughter being subject to that and have it brushed off as words I heard, 'heat of the moment' or they were 'all pumped up'," said Jackson, who played the South Australian Aussie rules competition in the late 1960.

"I think we see courage on the AFL field every weekend that transcends anything like two guys going toe-to-toe. That's silly, stupid and not courageous."

League officials introduced yet another crackdown on on-field fisticuffs, with referees boss Robert Finch suggesting Simpkins perhaps should have sent off Tallis.

"We now have a board directive on violence that needs to be passed onto the referees," Finch said. "That means referees will have the option of sending a player or players off or placing them on report.

"In most cases referees tend to take the safer option of reporting. Now if it is blatant violence I think they would send offenders off."

Literally days later, Josh Perry and Adrian Morley would trade blows after a scrum in a Friday night Knights-Roosters match. The following day in the Manly-Cowboys game halves Nathan Fien and Jason Ferris would also have a go. None of those players would be charged, because, as Gallop himself suggested, they were not as bad as the Tallis incident which went "beyond a scuffle". It was an indication that, once again, the league figured some punching was okay – a attitude that was no help to the referees.

The stoush between Gallop and Hall that started in the wake of the Tallis punch-up continued throughout the season. In May the NRL launched an investigation after Hall chose not to take any action on a spear tackle from Bulldog Ben Harris on Roosters winger Todd Byrne. Then in August came the surprising finding from a brawl in a Warriors-Broncos game in New Zealand. Referee Bill Harrigan sent four players to the sinbin, Commissioner Hall decided no further action was needed.

"It was unfortunate that judiciary commissioner Jim Hall decided not to single out any individual over the incident," Gallop said with the restraint of a lawyer. "Certainly we feel it would have been preferable had that occurred. The game can't accept that scenes like this are part of the sport."

In response Hall was unhappy Gallop didn't speak to him before making the comments. "I spoke to David earlier in the day but he didn't say anything about a press release going out and I'm disappointed in that," Hall said. "The referee handled the incident on the field well and penalised four players with stints in the sinbin and we thought that was sufficient."

By the end of the season Hall had figured out which way the wind was blowing. "When two blokes are involved in a fight and sent to the sinbin," he said in November 2003, "in the past that's been sufficient.

But times have changed, so we've got to go forward on that." The realisation would come too late to save Hall; Gallop had decided to split the commissioner's role in two and Hall was welcome to re-apply for his job. The NRL boss delivered the news to Hall while he was in a hospital bed recovering from back surgery. Hall didn't bother applying, figuring he had no chance of landing either of the new positions.

As for Ross and Tallis, the Panther would have the last laugh. They would bundle out the Tallis-captained Broncos in the first week of the 2003 finals 28-18 before going on to win the premiership.

<u>2005</u>
Trent Barrett Vs PJ Marsh

Sometimes, on-field punches can actually end up being a good thing. But you need a bit of perspective to see that. That's the case when Dragons captain Trent Barrett had a brain explosion and whacked Parramatta interchange player PJ Marsh in a Round 18 match at Parramatta Stadium.

There seems to have been a bit of a backstory to the second-half brainsnap. Ten minutes before half-time Barrett stayed down in a tackle with a sore neck after regathering a ball. To be honest, it doesn't look like there was anything wrong with the tackle at all, but the Dragons got the penalty. Marsh figured Barrett was milking it and, when the Dragons took the tap less than 10 metres from the Eels line, Marsh looked to be mocking Barrett – pointing at his own neck and shaking his head.

A few minutes later, Barrett tackles March with a bit more vigour than required, driving him backwards into the ground via his head and capping it off with a bit of a facial. These two incidents may well have set the scene for what happened in the second half.

The main event takes place at the 54th minute of a tight game, with the Eels up 16-14. Shaun Timmins gets tackled on the Dragons' side of halfway. Dummy half Albert Torrens flings the ball out to Barrett, who crosses the 40-metre line as he prepares to kick the ball downfield. On the TV coverage, almost as soon as he catches the ball, Marsh comes speeding into the frame from stage right, getting to Barrett just after the kick.

In attempting to charge down the kick, Marsh leaps into the air when he's just over a metre away. Instead of having his arms out to try and deflect the ball, both his arms are crossed and fists are clenched. Maybe he's bracing for contact, maybe not. Barrett certainly thinks not; while Marsh's elbow appears to hit him in the chest, Barrett takes the view he's been clocked in the face.

Knocked down – with a slow-motion "fuck" clearly seen spilling out of his mouth on the TV replay – Barrett has eyes only for Parramatta's No 14. As he regains his feet Barrett's left hand grabs Marsh's jersey from behind, his right clocks Marsh on the head. Then he holds him closer so as to get a better shot and flings another fist to the side of Marsh's head.

To be honest, Marsh looks more surprised than hurt by Barrett. But the Dragons captain isn't able to get any more punches going because damn near every player rushes in to join the fight/break it up (delete whichever motive is not applicable). This leaves the Dragons with a four-man defensive line, which is bad news in anyone's books.

Especially when the referee hasn't blown the whistle to stop play.

Down the other end, Eels fullback Wade Middleton fields the Barrett kick on his 20-metre line. With all four of those Dragons defenders on one side of the field, he heads to the gaping hole between centre-field and the sideline. Only one player seriously chases; the only other Dragon (it appears to be Luke Bailey) anywhere near Middleton opts to take his mouthguard out and give ref Tim Mander a spray.

Middleton clearly can't believe his good fortune; 30 metres out from the Dragons line, he slows down and looks back, seemingly expecting Mander to call a halt to proceedings. But Mander instead lets him touch down under the posts before asking the video referee to intervene.

In a textbook example of why you should play to the whistle, the guy in the booth sees nothing untoward in Marsh's challenge and awards the try. "Don't take matters into your own hands," Mander warns Barrett, "that's where you got yourself in trouble. We played the advantage – it's a try."

The conversion from right in front takes the score to 22-14. From the restart, the Dragons kick it dead and, as they say, the wheels start to fall off. What was a close game before Barrett's biff ends up a blowout. The Eels score 24 unanswered points after that incident to run out easy winners 40-14.

After the game, Barrett was not at all keen to talk about the incident. "I probably reacted and I shouldn't have," he admitted in the post-match press conference. "In the end it cost us. It was a little bit of ill-discipline from myself and I'd like to leave it at that."

Fat chance of that happening.

A day later, Marsh was in the papers, calling on the judiciary not to wuss out and let Barrett skate on by. "He's the captain of the side and is a prominent figure in the NRL and lots of kids look up to him. It's unacceptable to just go punching people, regardless of whether he's well thought of or not.

"I'm sure the NRL will look at it and I hope they don't go down the path of 'it's not in his nature', because that seems to be a lot of people's excuses at the moment."

While the Dragons said Barrett wouldn't be saying anything more about it, CEO Peter Doust decided to weigh in, saying the captain was "provoked" by Marsh. "In circumstances such as that, I'd be surprised if something didn't happen to the player who charged him down and hit him high."

And that's exactly what happened; what was

viewed on the field as okay was found by the judiciary to be worth a grade two careless high tackle charge. "It would have been handy to get that call on Friday night," Dragons lock Timmins ruefully said.

Barrett didn't escape either, being hit with a grade two striking charge. Marsh would plead guilty and dodge a suspension but Barrett would be outed for a week. Doust branded the whole event a "fiasco". "This is one of the most sensational set of circumstances I can recall involving our club and players," he said.

But this cloud would end up with a silver lining. Barrett's brain explosion seemed to be the catalyst that turned the Dragons season around. The loss to the Eels pushed them down into eighth spot, but they would win the remaining seven games of the season, finishing equal first with the Eels on 36 points.

The Dragons were pushed back to second on for-and-against, and would go all the way to the grand final decider, where they'd be knocked out by eventual premiers Wests Tigers. Though, without Barrett throwing those two punches, they might have missed the finals altogether. Despite the heartbreak that comes with falling one game short of the grand final, it's still better than already being on your end of season trip.

2008
Michael Weyman Vs Daniel Conn

Today Michael Weyman is a grand final winner and with a few Australian jerseys in his closet. But there was a time where, if you explained to someone this would happen, they'd have laughed at you. For once upon a time, Weyman was a player destined for a footy future of nothing special, due to a combination of injury and having a pair of itchy fists.

In Canberra, the forward made an unwanted name for himself as one who would over-react and fling a few punches. His short fuse was lit on at least three occasions, the first of which was a push-me-push-you affair between Jason Croker and Melbourne Storm's Matt King in 2006. And King had good reason to shape up to Croker; the Raider had just clipped Billy

Slater's legs as the fullback leapt to take a high ball. As Croker ran back to the defensive line, he bumped into King, who gave the forward a shove. One of those shoves that, in the world of rugby league means, "what the f..k did you do that for?".

In the world of rugby league the response to that shove – no matter how warranted it was – is to shove back. And so Croker shoves back and then they stare at each other for a few seconds, before both players realise the Storm already have the penalty and punching on would just make things worse. So they start to walk away.

Which is when Weyman flies into view from the right-hand side of the TV screen. Apparently not realising – or not caring – that the fight window has well and truly closed, he gives King a great shove with both hands. King grabs Weyman's jersey and flings a punch which, as far as the prop is concerned, is a case of "light blue touch paper and stand clear". The Raider then throws no fewer than seven straight right-handers into King's head before the other 24 players pile on and try to separate the pair.

The touchies come on and one tells referee Shayne Hayne that Weyman ran 10 metres to get involved in a fight that was over before he got there. So Hayne spreads his 10 fingers out in the direction of the grandstand and tells Weyman to get walking. Which he does, while shaking his head at the outrage of it all. For what it's worth, King gets 10 in the bin too.

A year later, Weyman was back at it again at Canberra Stadium, where the Raiders were killing the Eels. The game was effectively over by the 12-minute mark, with the scoreboard reading 24-0 to the home side. But Weyman would also be the focus of the game for two reasons. One would be the swinging arm that hit Eels prop Josh Cordoba in the head; Weyman would be put on report but, much to the later chagrin of Eels coach Michael Hagan (who said it was a "soft option" not to send him off), managed to stay on the field.

The second incident kicked off just after half-time, when renowned shitstirrer Mark Riddell started in on the fat jokes. Weyman had him by the jersey, pulling it over Riddell's head. The ref blew the whistle and

Weyman turned to protest the penalty. Then Riddell obviously said something, because Weyman spun around and immediately punched the rotund hooker. Which was a really big mistake; Riddell dropped the ball and then delivers close to a half-dozen straight rights and uppercuts.

Neither player would come clean on what words made Weyman see red but nearby Eels would suggest it might have been "Get off, you fat c..t". The Raiders prop would get sinbinned, Riddell seeing him off with one more jibe – "seeya fat boy" – before he too got 10 in the bin. "I know I don't have the best head as it is but I'm not going to let someone use it as a punching bag," Riddell said after the game.

Even though Riddell seemed to get far more punches in than Weyman, refs boss Robert Finch would suggest his sinbinning "a bit harsh". Weyman would escape any suspension for the fight but got two weeks to cool his heels for the high tackle.

A year later, the Weyman fists were flying again, in an incident that would lead to a great putdown from an opponent and would have the media doing its best to create a long-running feud. It would be Weyman's darkest time in footy, but out of the crap, would come salvation.

Weyman got cranky up on the sunny Gold Coast in 2008. With 15 minutes on the clock, the Raiders down 20-6, Weyman charged onto the ball like a forward who'd just come off the interchange bench. He was hit in a two-man Titans tackle, with forward and sometime model Daniel Conn up top. The guy called Horse didn't like something in the tackle and, after the play the ball, went for Conn at first marker. The Titans forward figured it was going to be one of those push and shove affairs, so he got a shock when Weyman hit the big green button marked "Go time!" and clocked him in the face. From that point both players threw a few more punches, with everyone else trying to pull them apart (and perhaps have a go themselves in the process).

After the stink subsided, referee Gavin Badger called the Raider over. "There was nothing in the tackle. You've king-hit the bloke. Go," he said, pointing to the sidelines, though by this stage of his career Weyman likely didn't need directions.

On the Fox Sports TV commentary, Andy Raymond couldn't believe the send-off at first. "Sent off for this?", he said incredulously, and then started to make his point, which seemed to be veering towards the 'it's a man's game. Next thing you know we'll be wearing skirts' argument. But then Raymond stopped dead when the bloodied face of Conn, his left eye already swollen shut, appeared on screen as he headed off to the blood bin. Okay, then. Send-off appropriate.

Raymond might have chosen to stay silent, but Conn was ready to let loose – verbally, I mean – when journalists put their microphones and recorders in front of him after full-time.

"I don't know what happened," he said. "I was in a tackle and just looked up and I thought he was just going to push me, but he seemed to have a bit of a brain snap. I looked away and closed my eyes … I thought he was going to push me but he king-hit me. He'll do his time for it. It was a bit of a low act but I'll leave it to the judiciary."

Raiders coach Neil Henry wasn't pleased, and neither was captain Alan Tongue. But Conn's teammates were fuming. Mark Minichiello branded it a "cheap shot" that broke Conn's nose and called for a minimum of six weeks on the sideline for Weyman. "I think we're all pretty dirty about it. I know I am. I kind of wish I was there at second marker."

It was opposing prop Luke Bailey who delivered the most devastating assessment of Weyman as a player. "He has a brain snap whenever he gets tired, which happens quite regularly," Bailey said. "He's only good for five to 10 minutes of the game. He always costs them [Canberra] more than he pleases them."

Former Canberra Raiders chief Kevin Neil – who let Weyman live at his house when he first arrived in the nation's capital – would jump to Weyman's defence. Though it would seem to be a bit of a knee-jerk response. Seemingly forgetting both the 2006 and 2007 fights, Neil said the Conn dust-up "would never happen unless he was highly provoked. He's never been sent off or anything like that." Weyman's manager Steve Stone also offered a less-than-ideal defence, saying "there was a stand-off and Michael just got in first" and "these things just happen". Yes, it "just happened" because Weyman threw a bunch of punches at Conn's head.

When the Raider fronted the judiciary, he got a five-week sentence for the fight and another week for a separate incident where he introduced his forearm to Titans centre Luke Dwyer's head.

Showing an impressive ability for honest self-assessment, Weyman actually agreed with Bailey's insults. "Maybe I am only a 10-minute [footballer]," he said. "In my time off I'm going to train as hard as I can and it's up to me to prove that wrong." He'd also offered a possible reason for his tendency to brawl; in an effort to shake off the "gentle giant" tag, Weyman has been trying to lift his on-field aggression. But he was lifting it too much. Way too much.

At this point in his career Weyman seemed destined to fade away into a footnote in the history of rugby league. Since his debut in 2003, the 23-year-old had played just 43 games thanks to the occasional suspension and a body prone to injury. Then new Dragons coach Wayne Bennett surprised the hell out of everyone and signed the suspended prop to a two-year deal. Bennett obviously saw something that no one else did, and the deal changed Weyman's career; he would go on to establish himself as a hard-running prop for St George Illawarra and earn NSW and Australian jerseys.

And, in 2010, he'd become a premiership winner in a grand final that saw him and Conn clash again – but in a way that caused many to scratch their heads.

Since 2008, they'd both switched clubs – Weyman to the Dragons and Conn to the Roosters. Thirty minutes into the grand final, with the Roosters up 8-6 and the Dragons looking very much like a team intent on losing yet another decider, Weyman took the ball up. Tackled by two players, he started going to ground. Which was when Conn and his left forearm came into the picture. Just before Weyman hit the turf, Conn's swinging arm clocked the forward on the top of the scone. The replays showed there was no doubt the arm came in contact with Weyman's bald dome; but they also showed what seemed to be a glancing blow. Yet Weyman's reaction suggested something else; he sat hunched forward on the field, loose-limbed like a kid's doll with his eyes rolling around in his head.

The trainer got Weyman him to his feet and then asked for assistance in taking him off the field; the forward dragging his feet as he walked to the sideline. It was all very odd; Conn's contact seemed so incidental that it was hard to fathom how it did so much damage to Weyman. And yet there didn't seem to be anything else going on in the tackle that would explain it.

Was Weyman foxing a bit? It's highly unlikely – Weyman had only just come back onto the field when it happened; it may have even been his first hit-up. Faking an injury to get off the field seconds after getting back on seems to be a strange tactic. Also, he never returned to the field in what was his first grand final. The match was 80 minutes long, but the club's top prop would be left on the sidelines watching most of it. So whatever went on in that 30th minute had genuinely rocked Weyman.

But Conn didn't see it that way. "He's a good actor," he said in the sheds after the game. "I don't think I even touched him. But, oh well, shit happens." The following year, when the pair met at in the 2011 Anzac Day clash, the media tried to build up the "feud", but Weyman wasn't having anything to do with that. "Oh, God no. I've moved on from everything. I've had enough of it. What's happened has happened and it's in the past." And it was – the newspaper coverage of the game made no mention of the pair having any sort of run-in.

In September 2013, Weyman played his last game – against the Warriors at WIN Stadium. In an interview with home-town paper the *Illawarra Mercury* ahead of the game, he offered the best explanation for his short-tempered days with the Raiders. "I guess before I came to the Dragons I was a frustrated footballer which is probably the reason I got sent off, suspended and all that kind of stuff. Things weren't looking really good. I was probably a bit sick of it and thought coming to the Dragons I would give it one last crack."

The premiership ring and the rep jerseys suggest it was a good move.

2011
Manly Vs Melbourne

Something got Adam Blair all feisty and riled up before what would be the infamous Round 25 Manly vs Melbourne clash. And it might have been coach Craig Bellamy. Over the previous few weeks, the forwards had lacked intensity in the first half of the game. At half-time in the previous week's game, Bellamy asked Blair to fire up for the second 40 - which he did. "We just wanted him to lead the way with our forwards," Bellamy told the media after their 8-6 win over the Dragons.

It's not hard to imagine Blair carried that instruction over to the following week into the start of what has gone down in history as the Battle of Brookvale (lucky it wasn't a Melbourne home game,

AAMI Park doesn't really lend itself to catchy fight-related names. The AAMI Park Punch-up just wouldn't have the same ring to it). Watching the match now and knowing what is going to happen at the 25th minute, you pay more attention to what's going on in those first 24 minutes, just looking for instances of niggle that helped the match boil over.

Doing that, you notice Adam Blair. There he is in the 20th minute, having an altercation with Darcy Lussick at the play the ball as the third man into a tackle, jamming his forehead into the face of the Manly interchange forward. A minute later, and he's copping a shove from Glenn Stewart, who resents Blair hitting him after he passed the ball. And in the 23rd minute, the normal calm and quite religious Brent Kite resents something in Blair's tackle, gets up and pushes him.

Between those second and third instances was a 10-minute stoppage when winger David Williams injured his shoulder while trying to score in the corner. Say what you will about Storm fullback Billy Slater (and I have said a few things in my time), he takes care of Williams. Slater was under Williams trying to stop him scoring. He quickly realised something was wrong and ends up cradling Williams like a big hairy baby. He even reaches down to grasp the winger's elbow to take the strain off his shoulder.

After such a long break in play, you might expect players (yes, I'm looking at you Adam Blair) might calm down a bit. But no. Blair got straight back into it; the Kite tackle was the very first after the restart of play.

And a tackle or two later the fuse is lit, courtesy of Storm forward Ryan Hinchcliffe's elbow. Hinchcliffe picked up a dropped ball in front of the Storm's uprights and charged forward. Lussick wrapped him up and the tackler copped an elbow to his jaw. Watching the game, it's hard to tell whether or not it was deliberate. Hinchcliffe does make direct contact with Lussick's face, which is a tick in the "deliberate" column, but he's not even looking at the tackler and may well have been trying to shrug him off, which we can mark down as "accidental".

Lussick certainly thought it was intentional; as he

gets up he gives Hinchcliffe a whack on the back of the head. The Storm forward doesn't take kindly to that and so the pair shape up, and moments of tension pass as they wonder who was going to throw the first bunch of fives.

Lussick, the answer is Lussick. He wasn't going to die wondering; reaching out with a left hand, he slaps Hinchcliffe on the cheek and then follows it with a short right to the centre of his face. It kicks off so quickly that Nine commentator Peter Sterling couldn't even finish the sentence "Lussick shapes up to Hinchcliffe" before the slap and the punch are thrown.

"This is all pretty extraordinary," Phil Gould rightly notes in the commentary. "There was a little bit of push and shove and then all of a sudden, they let them go."

You'll note that, as of this point, Adam Blair is nowhere to be seen. But he makes an appearance quite soon after the pair start brawling. With Storm players milling about trying to break up the fight, Blair enters from stage left like a missile. After the ref calls time out, Nine shows a reverse angle of the huddle of players, where we can see what Blair does after he races in – he throws a right-handed uppercut in the vicinity of Lussick's head.

Glenn Stewart enters the frame from the right and makes a beeline for Blair. While the footage is unclear, there is a wave of movement from the vicinity of the pair, suggesting some punches were let loose somewhere in that huddle. The two are the last to break away, remaining in a bear hug as if trying to restrain the other from throwing a punch.

The touch judges come on and they sort things out with referee Shayne Hayne. Hinchcliffe gives up the penalty for the elbow, and then they deal with Stewart and Blair. The former gets 10 in the bin for running in to get involved and he's sent to the sideline.

Blair is standing there, listening to everything that's been said. And you can tell he knows he's heading to the bin too. He's almost heading off before Hayne puts those 10 fingers in the air.

Given what is about to kick off, this is the instant where the Monday morning quarterbacks would say

Hayne screwed up. When he sent Blair to the bin, they say, he should have waited until Stewart had left the field. It's an unfair criticism – as is any criticism made with the benefit of hindsight. But the reality is he *does* wait – almost 15 seconds passes from the time Stewart starts his dawdle from the field to the sheds to when he tells Blair to get going.

That's plenty of time for someone to walk off. Besides Stewart is just a metre from the sideline when the jogging Blair catches up to him. If Hayne waited for Stewart to walk that extra metre before binning Blair, the Storm forward would still have caught him before he got to the sheds, and what happens next would still have happened.

What happens next is words are exchanged (Stewart insisted Blair called him a rude word while Blair said Stewart started the verbal jousting) and then Stewart looks over his shoulder, as if to locate the referee in the centre of the field. As he turns his head back, he discovers Blair has grabbed a handful of his jersey. So Stewart punches him.

And things go crazy. Stewart's brother Brett flies

in to try and grab Blair but misses (and probably sustains an injury that would see him miss the second half of the match), and two team-mates follow him. From there, the entirety of both teams rush to the brawl (even a reluctant Slater who, in a wide shot is shown to be the last person to start running in. It's almost like he thought "everyone else is in, I guess I *have to* go too") Of particular concern is the sighting of several Storm players in warm-up jackets getting hands-on in the brawl.

Once things calm down, Stewart and Blair resume their walks to the sheds. Which was a bit of a waste of time, because Hayne had to call both of them back out to inform them they were gone for the whole game; as a result of the sideline scuffle they were both sent off. No-one else receives any on-field punishment, but Hayne would place the whole incident on report so that the review committee could exercise their fast-forward, rewind and pausing skills as they scanned through footage of the brawl.

It almost feels incidental, but the Sea Eagles went on to win the match 18-4. Would have been 18-blot but for a scrappy Slater try six seconds from time.

In coverage of the brawl over the coming days, many would bring up the 1985 Test tussle between Australia's Greg Dowling and New Zealander Kevin Tamati, but that fight was just between the two of them. Not a single player left the field to join them, they all stood on the sidelines and watched. Also, the one-week suspension copped by Dowling and Tamati would be nothing compared to the punishments handed out after the Battle of Brookvale.

NRL boss David Gallop was at the game, which was interesting timing. It was the first time he'd attended a Storm game since he rubbed them out for cheating the gap, and his first Sea Eagles match since suspending Brett Stewart for four games at the start of the 2009 season for being charged with sexual misconduct (he was later acquitted in court).

As you might expect the head honcho wasn't too pleased with what he saw. "The biff has got no place in the game and people who say that it does, that's nonsense. Our game is so tough, you only have to go into a dressing room at the end of our games and see what our players have been through to know that we don't need this in our game to call it a tough game."

One of those who disagreed was none other than Les Boyd, who had been dining at Dapto Leagues Club with the game on the TV screens. "The club was chock-a-block and the punters went off," Boyd said. "You've never heard noise and cheering like it and it got louder when they kept replaying it." He understood why this sort of thing couldn't take place in the modern game, but felt sorry for the players who had to deal with biff-free rugby league. "They train and they're told to beat the shit out of each other, yet the NRL penalises them when things get a bit out of hand."

In the fallout from the brawl, Manly CEO David Perry became one of those people who chose to blame Hayne for not possessing the magical ability to see into the future. "They need to put something in place," he said, "where touch judges could individually take these players a reasonable distance off the field, where club officials can take over and escort them to the sheds."

Because, you know, it's not as if it's the players' responsibility to avoid punching on.

Dragons coach Wayne Bennett was one of the few who saw sense, rightly blaming the players, not the referee. "At the end of the day, if guys want to fight it doesn't matter how you send them off or what you do with them," he said. "They have got to be accountable. We just keep blaming someone else."

The league would adjust the rules so that a player had to cross the sideline before the referee gave another their marching orders (though, given that Stewart was at the sideline when the brawl started, it's hard to see how this rule would have changed things at Brookvale that night).

All 34 players – including those who rushed off the bench – were going to be held accountable, with the NRL combing through video to see just how many it would punish. The Storm got in early with some damage control, releasing a printed apology from Adam Blair (which you just know was actually written by a club official). "It was a spur of the moment reaction that was not planned and to be honest it happened that quickly I still don't really know why it occurred," Blair 'said'. "I'm extremely disappointed to be involved in such an incident that does not put the game in a positive light."

Blair and Glenn Stewart were guaranteed to win a trip to the judiciary, and eight other players were spotted doing the wrong thing. Lussick, who started the whole thing, copped a contrary conduct charge, as did team-mates Brett Stewart, Kieran Foran and Michael Robertson. From the Storm, the finger of fate pointed at bench players Sisa Waqa, Sika Manu, Brian Norrie and Jaiman Lowe. It was the largest number of players charged from a single game since the league began in 1908.

On top of the certainty of losing players through suspension, the league whacked both teams with a $50,000 fine. The Storm's bench players would all miss a week, as would Brett Stewart and Foran, with Lussick cooling his heels for three weeks (Robertson would avoid any suspension).

Blair would be gone for five weeks – three for the sideline brawl and two for the earlier on-field punches. This was despite his legal rep Geoff Bellew describing the sideline stink as a three-second fight as far as his client was concerned. "He's not charged with inciting a riot, he's not charged with running in," Bellew told the judiciary. "He was charged with being in a fight. The fight with which he's charged lasts three seconds - from the time he and Glenn Stewart came together to the time the third man came in."

His opponent had to wait another day to find out his fate, after his lawyer pulled out the night of the judiciary. If it was a stunt to gain a reduced sentence, it didn't work – Stewart would get three weeks for the brawl as well. Before the sentence, he would give his version of events to the judiciary. As he was walking to the sideline, he said he turned to see what was happening to Blair. "I wanted to keep an eye on where he was," Stewart said. "I didn't want to have my back to him the whole time. I thought he was running around me ... he said 'come on, let's go', then a swear word – I can't really remember what swear word. He said something, the swear word offended me. He had a go at me, and it escalated from there."

Wow, must have been *some* swear word.

The three-week suspension worked out well for Stewart. His first game back would end up being the grand final, where the Sea Eagles would beat the Warriors 24-10. The suspension sucked for Tim Robinson, though. He was the guy who had to make way for Stewart's return to the 17, missing what would his only shot to play in a top grade grand final.

The events of that Friday night in August 2011 would cement the Manly-Melbourne rivalry in many people's minds and they'd wait for a similar explosion whenever the teams met up. That explosion would occur seven years later at AAMI Park when Curtis Scott, sick of being riled up by serial niggler Dylan Walker, let fly with the fists. He landed a few to Walker's face – one of which closed up an eye – and became the first player sent off in three years. Walker and team-mate Apisai Koroisau would each get 10 in the bin for their part in the tussle – and there would be controversy when they returned to the field almost two minutes early due to a time-keeping error.

There must have been something in the air that

round – 14 players got 10 in the bin. Though only Scott was marched.

<u>2013</u>
Paul Gallen Vs Nate Myles

"Is that the best you've got? C'mon then. Let's go."

Those 10 words – or something very similar – have likely prefaced many an on-field altercation since rugby league began in 1908. But when those words were uttered at the middle on ANZ Stadium just seconds before half-time one night in early June 2013, they sparked a huge change in the game. Not in the rules, but in the way they were applied.

Those words fell from the mouth of Queenslander Nate Myles and were directed at the polarising figure of Paul Gallen. Come Origin time, the one-time Sharks caption was Public Enemy No1 in Queensland. The rest of the year, well, he had a lot of detractors in NSW as well. Whether it's racially abusing someone, tearing at the fresh stitches from an opponent's wound, allegedly squirrel-gripping another, slapping an unconscious player in the face, the Sharks drug and salary cap scandals, there are more than enough reasons for some to be members of the I Hate Paul Gallen fan club. Though, it should be said, he's unlikely to care about that.

Some of the above instances would tend to illustrate Gallen from time to time shows some poor decision-making skills on the field. It was much the same deal in the 39th minute of Game One in the 2013 State of Origin series. NSW had the wood on Queensland in the first half, leading 14-0. The Maroons were looking a bit lost and needing some motivation.

And that's just what Gallen did; with his team in control, he effectively gave the other side a leg up. For the previous few years, Gallen and the rest of the NSW camp had been quietly seething about Myles' tactics that included leading with the head in some tackles or twisting players' legs.

With the game clock 15 seconds into the final minute of the first half, Myles carts it up to be hit by Luke Lewis and Anthony Watmough. Even though they have it all in hand, Gallen sees Myles' exposed head and, in his own words, "tried to cheap shot Nate by swinging my right arm heavily into him. My forearm hit him just under his chin."

Myles gets up, plays the ball and then – with a smile on his face – gives Gallen a shove. It's here where he uttered those words that opened this chapter, the words that Gallen couldn't resist. While the play goes on towards the sideline, the two have the briefest of Mexican standoffs, until Gallen tires of waiting and lets fly with a left jab into Myles jaw, followed by a right and an uppercut.

"Oh, there's a punch-up in the centre of the ground," Ray Warren says in the call. "Nate Myles with a left and right from Gallen and they both landed. They both landed flush."

Well, of course they both landed. They came out of the blue for Myles, who had his hands down by his side for the first punch. As the second hits, Myles appears to be reeling and reaches out to grab Gallen's jersey to stop himself from hitting the deck. Gallen gets that uppercut away as players from both sides rush in. To be frank, it's doubtful whether Myles even throws a single punch.

Curiously, it's Gallen's swinging arm rather than

the punches that earns Queensland a penalty. As referee Ashley Klein is disciplining him, Gallen makes sure to get his side of the story in. "He is getting my knee and twisting it every time. He's been doing it series after series, headbutting and twisting."

In reference to the punches, Klein tells Gallen, "what happens next, we're not going to tolerate. Don't start now." And yet he receives no on-field punishment, suggesting the referees are in fact going to tolerate that.

In the second half, NSW would not score again, while Queensland would score a try (and have a second disallowed) to go down 14-6. The Queensland side that was lost in the first half had found their motivation in the second. And they would carry that through to Game II, where they'd be up 24-0 before NSW scored their first points at the 70th minute.

Blues coach Laurie Daley didn't see anything wrong with what he tagged a "great Origin moment"; to him Gallen was sticking up for his team-mates. "I'd be disappointed if anything came out of it," he said. "I thought it was a tough, brutal, hard game of footy."

Ex-Maroon player Steve Renouf saw it differently, labelling it as a "bit of a dog act". "Nate Myles was standing there," Renouf said, "and *bang bang*. You just don't do that, you know?". Former referee Bill Harrigan said Gallen had crossed a line and should have been binned. "Nate Myles was standing there looking at him, and he just unloaded with those two shots. You just can't do that."

But the man on the receiving end didn't have a problem with it (perhaps, in part, because he figured *something* would eventually be coming his way for all that twisting and headbutting).

"Let's be honest, everyone wants to see it," Myles told the *Sydney Morning Herald* of his experience as a punching bag. "I don't think he should get charged. That's just the way it goes. To be honest I'd leave it on the field. That's Origin."

The debate on the merits of the punches would continue through the week. Robbie Farah, the Blues hooker in the 2012 series, claimed he had been victim of Myles' headbutt tackling style, while the Queensland journos would list Gallen's rap sheet to show that it was he and not Myles who was the real bully.

Gallen would miss a week of club footy after pleading guilty to a striking charge. During his week on the sideline he would join the chorus of suspended players and point out the hypocrisy of criticising punch-ups while also using them to promote the game. "I feel pretty dudded that I have to sit out a week because of a fight in Origin when you look at all the promotions promoting Origin – they're stinks," Gallen said on Peter Sterling's *Sterlo* TV show. "I hope the NRL step in now and don't allow that footage to be used to promote the game."

It's something that has always been a fair point to raise. Though it's more often the broadcaster and sports reporters who use biff to promote a big game, while also decrying the players for taking part at the same time. In this case, while the NRL ruled out using the footage in a promotional sense, the Nine Network hedged its bets.

Nine's head of sport Steve Crawley pointed out that it had been on the back page of NSW and Queensland newspapers for days. "So it's an issue," he said. "It's something people are talking about. We have to be reflective of that. We don't want to highlight violence, but at the moment this is an issue people are talking about. We haven't decided yet, but it's not going away."

A week and a half out from Game II, the league dropped a bombshell. It had had enough and decided any punches would earn the thrower a stint in the bin. After more than 100 years of efforts to deal with on-field violence, the league finally worked out that to stamp it out all they had to do was enforce the rules. After all, there's never been anything in the rule book that said players were allowed to punch each other.

At the core of the decision was the simple fact that it was a bad look for the game. "We need to make sure our game can recruit young kids," said NRL referees boss Daniel Anderson. "We've got a duty to the community and to people involved in our sport. There are a lot of swinging voters on our game who could be turned away by certain incidents."

And of course some bleated that the game was becoming soft, that it would lose something if you took away a player's ability to punch an opponent in the head. Fight fan and former Maroon Chris Close complained the league had caved in to the "do gooders". "The game's been going for over 100 years and I don't think there's been anyone really badly hurt by a punch," he said. Really? Perhaps he should go talk to Steeler Lee Pomfret, whose career was cut short by that 1982 punch from Bob Cooper.

Gallen, of course, was no fan of a law that would stop him punching people. "I think it's getting sanitised too much," Gallen said in a Triple M radio interview. He pledged not to do it again, "because I don't want to get a 10-minute stint in the sin bin". Exactly, that's the whole point of the rule change; to alter the behaviour of a serial offender.

The very next Origin game provided evidence to support the argument that players can be slow on the uptake. In the second half of a game that had well and truly gotten away from the Blues (the score was 18-0 at the time) NSW forward Trent Merrin had a massive over-reaction to Brent Tate pushing Gallen off the tackled Johnathan Thurston. Standing at marker, Merrin awkwardly shuffled towards Tate and gave him a few fives to the face. "Now, some punches," Ray Warren said on the commentary like he'd been waiting the whole game for them.

Players of both sides rushed in, including Justin Hodges, who loves a fight as long as he has some forwards to back him up, and Greg Bird, who just loves a fight. The fight broke up into three distinct groups, with most players doing nothing more than jersey tugging.

After the red mist lifted, the referees had to enforce the new rule. And they mucked it up a bit. Tate got 10 in the bin, despite not seeming to throw a single punch. Hodges went next, a smile on his face saying he knew exactly what was coming. After those two got their marching orders, it was clear Merrin was gone, and Bird followed him soon afterwards. (though he also claimed he'd not hit anyone).

At the end of the day, the league had warned the players what would happen if they punched on. And yet the players punched on. But of course some camps complained; how ridiculous would it be, they said, if there were seven or eight players fighting and they were all binned? It was an argument that missed the obvious fact that the new law would take some time to be bedded down, before players realised they'd be gone for 10 for fighting.

Some would be slower to learn that others. Merrin, who copped a week's suspension, said he wouldn't stop throwing punches. "I'm not going to hold back if one of my mates or myself are getting punched in the head," he told the *Sydney Morning Herald*.

But they would all learn. A year on from the edict

being handed down, fights had all but disappeared from the game. "I don't think it's changed the product," said Maroons forward Corey Parker. "You can have a cracking game of football without a fight."

Nate Myles realised the tide had turned. "When it was all about the fans, they just wanted to see a free-for-all," he told the *Herald*. "It's not that way anymore. It's about changing the image and players have to be responsible for that."

As for the guy who started it all, well, it seemed he was taking a bit longer to get there. "I think it's embarrassing when blokes run in and grab each other and push and pull," Gallen said a year after his stink that changed the game. "That looks worse than a fight in my opinion."

BIBLIOGRAPHY

Plenty of newspaper articles were used in the preparation of *Biff*. They were sourced via various newspaper archives, including the utterly invaluable online source Trove (without which the Earl Park Riot and NSW/England clash would have been impossible to write). Rather than include each article in the bibliography individually, I've chosen to list the publications instead.

Books

Adams, Tony, *Masters of the Game*, Ironbark, 1996

Andrews, Malcolm, *Hardmen*, Allen & Unwin, 2012

Apter, Jeff, *The Coaches: The Men Who Changed Rugby League*, Five Mile Press, 2014

Arthurson, Ken and Heads, Ian, *Arko: My Game*, Pan Macmillan, 1997

Buckler, Rick, *That's Entertainment: My Life in The Jam*, Omnibus, 2015

Cashman, Richard (ed), *Tales from Coathanger City: Ten Years of Tom Brock Lectures*, Australian Society for Sports History and Tom Brock Bequest Committee, 2010

Chesterton, Ray, *Manly Sea Eagles: The Team They Love To Hate*, New Holland 2016

Collis, Ian, and, Whiticker, Alan, *The History of Rugby League Clubs*, New Holland, 2014

Collis, Ian, and Whiticker, Alan, *Rugby League Through the Decades*, New Holland, 2011

Gorman, Joe, *Heartland: How Rugby League Explains Queensland*, University of Queensland Press, 2019

Haddan, Steve, *The Finals: 100 Years of National Rugby League Finals*, Steve Haddan, 1992

Heads, Ian, and Middleton, David, *A Centenary of Rugby League 1908-2008*, Pan MacMillan, 2008

Heads, Ian, *Saints: The Legend Lives On*, Playright Publishing, 2001

Hewitt, Paolo, *Paul Weller: The Changing Man*, Bantam, 2007

Hauser, Liam, *State of Origin: 35 Years*, Rockpool Publishing, 2015

Masters, Roy, *Bad Boys, Random House, 2010*

Masters, Roy, *Inside League*, Pan Books, 1990

Middleton, David (ed), *Rugby League Week: 25 Sensational Years*, HarperSports, 1995

Piggins, George, *Never Say Die: The Fight to Save the Rabbitohs*, Pan MacMillan, 2001

Reilly, Malcolm (with Ian Heads), *A Life in League*, Ironbark, 1998

Whiticker, Alan, and Collis, Ian, *101 Great Rugby League Players*, New Holland, 2012

Whiticker, Alan, *Mud, Blood and Beer: Rugby League in the 1970s*, New Holland, 2014

Whiticker, Alan, and Hudson, Glen, *The Encyclopedia of Rugby League Players*, Gary Allen, 1999

Newspapers and magazines

Big League
Brisbane Telegraph
Brisbane Truth
Courier-Mail
Daily Advertiser
Daily Examiner
Illawarra Mercury
Mirror
Newcastle Morning Herald
Newcastle Sun
Rugby League Week
Sun

Glen Humphries

Sunday Mail
Sun-Herald
Sydney Morning Herald
Sydney Sportsman
Sydney Truth
Telegraph
Townsville Daily Bulletin
Truth

Lightning Source UK Ltd.
Milton Keynes UK
UKHW040701160921
390675UK00001B/62

9 780648 032397